NEW Cornerstone

STUDENT EDITION
with Digital Resources

Pearson

New Cornerstone 3

Pearson, 221 River Street, Hoboken, NJ 07030
Cover credit: Alphaspirit/123RF

Library of Congress Cataloging-in-Publication Data
A catalog record for the print edition is available from the Library of Congress.

The publishers would like to recognize the contributions of our original Series Consultants, Anna Uhl Chamot, Jim Cummins, and Sharroky Hollie. This edition is published in memory of Dr. Chamot, an extraordinary educator, writer, and scholar.

Printed in the United States of America
ISBN-10: 0-13-523271-6 (with Digital Resources)
ISBN-13: 978-0-13-523271-2 (with Digital Resources)
1 18

www.english.com/cornerstone

Consultants and Reviewers

Carlos Eduardo Aguilar Cortés
Universidad Andes
Bogotá, Colombia

Rebecca Anselmo
Sunrise Acres Elementary School
Las Vegas, NV, USA

Ana Applegate
Redlands School District
Redlands, CA, USA

Terri Armstrong
Houston ISD
Houston, TX, USA

Jacqueline Avritt
Riverside County Office of Ed.
Hemet, CA, USA

Mitchell Bobrick
Palm Beach County School
West Palm Beach, FL, USA

Victoria Brioso-Saldala
Broward County Schools
Fort Lauderdale, FL, USA

Brenda Carbarga Schubert
Creekside Elementary School
Salinas, CA, USA

Gabriela Diaz
Grilli Canning College
Buenos Aires, Argentina

Joshua Ezekiel
Bardin Elementary School
Salinas, CA, USA

Valeria Goluza
Grilli Canning College
Buenos Aires, Argentina

Veneshia Gonzalez
Seminole Elementary School
Okeechobee, FL, USA

Carolyn Grigsby
San Francisco Unified School District
San Francisco, CA, USA

Julie Grubbe
Plainfield Consolidated Schools
Chicago, IL, USA

Yasmin Hernandez-Manno
Newark Public Schools
Newark, NJ, USA

Do Thi Thanh Hien
The Asian International School
Ho Chi Minh City, Vietnam

Janina Kusielewicz
Clifton Public Schools/Bilingual Ed.
& Basic Skills Instruction Dept.
Clifton, NJ, USA

Mary Helen Lechuga
El Paso ISD
El Paso, TX, USA

Jose Augusto Lugo
Cerros
Bogotá, Colombia

Gayle P. Malloy
Randolph School District
Randolph, MA, USA

Le Tue Minh
Wellspring International Bilingual
School
Hanoi, Vietnam

Minh Phuong Nguyen
CIEM-Education
Hanoi, Vietnam

Patricia Parroquiano
Gimnasio Campestre Reino Britanico
Bogota, Colombia

Randy Payne
Patterson/Taft Elementaries
Mesa, AZ, USA

Maria Eugenia Pérez de Castro
Escuela Primaria Puerta Abierta
Buenos Aires, Argentina

Carolina Pérez Martínez
Thomas Jefferson School
Xalapa, Mexico

Lucy Reyes
Colegio Axis
Mexicali, B.C., Mexico

Sergio Rivera
Liceo Hermano Miguel La Salle
Bogota, Colombia

Marcie L. Schnegelberger
Alisal Union SD
Salinas, CA, USA

Delphine Sichler
Keystone International Education
Córdoba, Mexico

Lorraine Smith
Collier County Schools
Naples, FL, USA

Shawna Stoltenborg
Glendale Elementary School
Glen Burnie, MD, USA

Kampanart Thammaphati
Wattana Wittaya Academy
Thailand

Hoang Dieu Thu
Edison Schools
Vietnam

Denise Tiffany
West High School
Iowa City, IA, USA

Classroom Language

Teacher	Student
Come in.	I don't understand.
Sit down.	I don't know.
Sit in a circle.	Please could you help me?
Stand up.	Please can you repeat that?
Listen carefully.	What page are we on?
Please be quiet.	How do you spell … ?
Please open your book to page … .	How do you pronounce … ?
Turn to page 12.	How do you say … in English?
Look at the board.	Is this correct?
Work in pairs. / Works in groups.	I have finished.
Repeat after me.	May I go to the restroom?
Put your books / things away.	Please may I open the window?
Close the door, please.	I'm sorry I'm late.

Welcome to **New Cornerstone**!

We wrote **New Cornerstone** to help you succeed in all your school studies. This program will help you learn the English language you need to study language arts, social studies, math, and science. You will learn how to speak to family members, classmates, and teachers in English.

New Cornerstone includes a mix of many subjects. Each unit has three different readings that include some fiction (made-up) and nonfiction (true) articles, stories, songs, and poems. The readings will give you some of the tools you need to do well in all your subjects in school.

As you use this program, you will build on what you already know and learn new words, new information and facts, and take part in creative activities. The activities will help you improve your English skills.

Learning a language takes time, but just like learning to skateboard or learning to swim, it is fun!

We hope you enjoy **New Cornerstone**, and we wish you success on every step of your learning journey.

Communities

Unit Preview

Reading 1: Literature / Poem

Reading 2: Literature / Short Story

Reading 3: Literature / Personal Narrative

Put It All Together

Meeting Challenges

Reading 3: Informational Text / Social Studies

Put It All Together

Animals in Nature

Great Ideas

 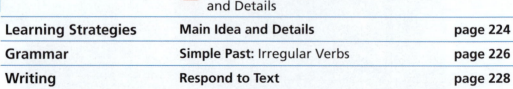

Reading 3: Informational Text / Photo Essay

Contents

Neighbors in Space

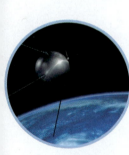

Reading 3: Informational Text / Biography

Put It All Together

Unit 6

Contents

Art for Everyone

Reading 3: Informational Text / Newspaper Article

Put It All Together

Unit 1

Communities

Your community is where you live with your family. It is where you play with your friends and go to school.

Reading 1
Poem

Lin's Shopping Day

Reading 2
Short Story

Making Friends

Reading 3
Narrative

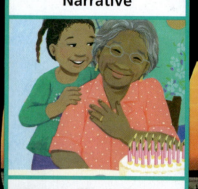

My Family

THE BiG QUESTION

What are some ways that communities are alike and different?

Listening and Speaking

You will talk about what children do in different communities. In the Listening and Speaking Workshop, you will play a descriptive guessing game.

Writing

You will practice descriptive writing. In the Writing Workshop, you will write a description of an event.

Quick Write

Do you like where you live? Write three reasons why you like your community.

View and Respond

Talk about the poster for this unit. Then watch and listen to the video and answer the questions at Pearson English Portal.

Build Unit Vocabulary

What do you know about communities?

Words to Know

Listen and repeat. Use these words to talk about people who work in your community.

bus driver   **police officer**   **mail carrier**   **teacher**

Practice

Work with a partner. Look up the verbs in a dictionary.
Then ask and answer questions.

teaches us	protects us	brings us mail	drives a bus

Example: A: What does a <u>police officer</u> do?

B: A <u>police officer protects us</u>.

Write

Read the question. Write your response in your notebook.

What do you want to be when you grow up?

Make Connections

Complete the sentences.

bus stop

police station

school

post office

1. Some police officers work at the _____,
   and others work outside.

2. We go to _____ every day, and so do our
   teachers, the principal, and the rest of the staff.

3. We can give our mail to a mail carrier, or we can take it to
   the _____.

4. You can catch a bus at a bus station or at a
   _____.

What about you?

Look at the jobs below. Talk about what each one does.
Where do they work?

doctor   firefighter   cook

Kids' Stories from around the World 🎧

U.S.A.

Chile

Chris

My family and I live in a suburb. The suburb is near a big city in Illinois. A suburb has many houses. My friends and I take the yellow bus to go to school. In the afternoon, we do our homework. Then all the children play outside.

Lucia

My family and I live in a small town in the Andes. The Andes are mountains in Chile. There is no school in my town. I go to a school in another town. It is thirty miles away! The ride to school is long, but I love living in the mountains.

China

South Africa

Gen

I live in a big city called Shanghai. Shanghai is in China. My family lives in a tall apartment building. My sister and I take the bus to go to school. The city is busy in the morning.

Mandisa

I am from South Africa. I live on my family's farm. We grow strawberries. There are other farms near us. All the children get together in the morning to go to school. We help around the farm, too.

What about you?

1. What kind of community do you live in?

2. How do you get to school? Share your story.

What You Will Learn

Reading
- Vocabulary building: *Context, phonics*
- Reading strategy: *Understand character*
- Text type: *Literature (poem)*

Grammar
Simple present: *be* verbs

Writing
Describe a person

These words will help you understand the reading.

Key Words

- street
- flower
- luck
- letter
- greet

Key Words

Lin's Shopping Day is a poem about a girl going around her neighborhood.

Words in Context 🎧

1 The mail carrier is holding **letters**.

2 There are a lot of people on the **street**.

③ What **luck**! The ball is in my glove!

④ I give my grandmother **flowers**.

⑤ They **greet** each other.

Practice

Create a vocabulary notebook.

- Divide your page into three columns: the new words, their definitions, and drawings of the words when possible.
- Test yourself by covering one of the columns.

Make Connections

Lin likes to walk around town with her dad. What do you like to do in your community? Why? Discuss. Use some of the key words as you speak.

W B
3

These words will help you talk about the reading.

Academic Words

item
single piece or thing

purchase
buy

Academic Words

Words in Context

I have a list of new words. The first **item** on my list is *communities*.

You can **purchase** a book at a bookstore.

Practice

Choose an academic word to complete each sentence.

1. We go to the post office to _____ stamps for our letters.

2. I have a list of things to do today. The first _____ on my list is to play soccer with my friends.

Apply

Write the answers in your notebook. Use the academic words. Then ask and answer with a partner.

1. What is one **item** your family usually buys at the store?

2. Do you usually get books from the library, or do you **purchase** them?

4

Phonics

Short Vowels

The **vowels** are *a, e, i, o,* and *u.* The other letters are called **consonants**. The words in the chart have short vowels. Listen. Then read each word aloud.

can	bed	sit	top	bus

Rule

A word may have a short vowel when:
- the word has just one vowel.
- the word has a consonant before and after the vowel.

c a t   p u p
C V C   C V C

Practice

Work with a partner. Take turns.

- Read the sentences.
- Find the words with the CVC pattern.

1. Gus drives the bus.

2. The cat is big.

3. The girls sit on the bed.

4. Do not pick up the pup.

5

Literature
Poem

🎧 **Listen to the Audio.**
Listen for the general meaning. Use the pictures to help you understand the selection.

Reading Strategy

Understand Character

As you read, think about the main character, Lin:

- What does she do?
- What kind of person is she? Find clues.

Listen as your teacher models the reading strategy.

Lin's Shopping Day

Lin jumps from the bus onto the street.
With so many people, she must move her feet.
Dad quickly takes hold of Lin's little hand.
The first stop on their list is a smelly fish stand.

Lin **takes a sniff** and pinches her nose.
She can see lobsters if she stands on her toes.
Next on their list is a store that sells <mark>flowers</mark>.
Lin tells Dad she could smell them for hours.

Next they stop to buy bok choy.
It's a type of cabbage that brings Mom joy.
Inside the market they see Mr. Brown.
Lin says it's <mark>luck</mark> to see her teacher in town.

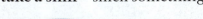

take a sniff   smell something

Reading Skill

To understand the phrase *take a sniff*, read the definition.

Before You Go On

How does Lin feel about the city?
How do you know?

They wave hello and stop to talk,
then say good-bye at the end of the block.
Lin turns the corner without looking around.
CRASH! The mail carrier's letters are all over the ground.

Lin says she's sorry and helps him repack.
Then Dad says it's time to go buy a snack.
They go to the candy store for a sweet treat.
Lin sees a police officer she stops to greet.

Reading Skill

The words *street* and *greet* are key words for this reading.

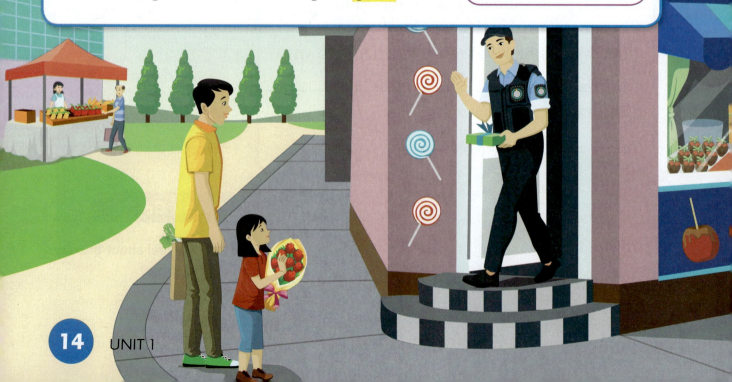

Finally, it's time to get home to Mom.
If they're late, Mom won't be **calm**.
So Dad and Lin stop and wait for the bus.
"Look," says Lin, "the driver remembers us!"

---

calm   relaxed, not mad

Reading Strategy

Understand Character

Looking for clues can help you learn
about a character.

- What clues help you learn what
  Lin is like?

- How did looking for clues help you
  learn about Lin?

Think It Over

1. **Recall** What items
   do Lin and her father
   purchase?

2. **Comprehend** How does
   Lin help people in her
   community?

3. **Analyze** How do you
   think people feel about
   Lin?

6–8

Learning Strategies

Understand Character

A **character** is a person in a story or poem. You can learn about characters by what they say or do.

Practice

Read each sentence. Then choose the word that tells what Lin is like.

> **a.** helpful   **b.** busy
> **c.** nice   **d.** friendly

1. _____ Lin greets a police officer.
2. _____ Lin goes to the fish market, the flower shop, and the vegetable stand.
3. _____ Lin repacks the mail.
4. _____ Lin buys bok choy for Mom.

Use a Character Web

You can use a Character Web to tell what a person is like.

GO 14

Practice

Tell what Lin does. Use the questions below to help you. Tell what Lin is like. The first one is done for you.

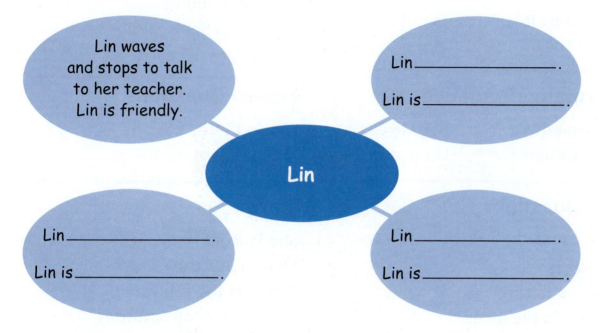

Lin waves and stops to talk to her teacher. Lin is friendly.

Lin_____.
Lin is_____.

Lin

Lin_____.
Lin is_____.

Lin_____.
Lin is_____.

1. Which actions tell you that Lin is helpful?
2. How do you know that Lin likes to be busy?
3. How do you know that Lin is happy?

9

Apply

Retell the poem to a partner. You can refer to the pictures as you speak.

Extension

Who is your favorite community helper? Give the person's name and say why he or she is your favorite.

Grammar

Simple Present: *Be* Verbs

Different Forms of *Be*

Subject	be	
I	**am**	
You	**are**	nice.
He / She / It	**is**	
We / They	**are**	

I**'m** / You**'re**
He**'s** / She**'s** / It**'s**
We**'re** / They**'re**

Affirmative/Negative

Affirmative		Negative
Lin **is** there.	→	Lin **is not** there.

Yes/No Questions

Is Lin there? Yes, she **is**.
No, she **is not.**

Wh- Questions

Who is Lin?	She **is** a girl.
What is that?	That **is** bok choy.
Where is Lin?	She **is** at the fish stand.
When is the game?	The game **is** on Saturday.
Why is Lin happy?	She **is** happy to shop.

Practice A

**Rewrite the sentences in your notebook. Make them negative.
Use contractions.**

1. The picture is pretty. The picture isn't pretty.

2. He is a good baseball player.

3. We are helpful.

4. He is a nice boy.

Practice B

Answer each question. Use *yes* or *no*. Write it in your notebook.

1. Are Lin and Dad happy? (yes) Yes, they are.

2. Is Lin sad? (no)

3. Is Mr. Brown nice? (yes)

4. Are the letters on the ground? (yes)

5. Are you calm? (no)

Apply

**Work with a partner. Ask and answer the questions.
Use *be* verbs in your answers.**

Example: A: What is your favorite color?

B: My favorite color is blue.

- What is your name?
- When is your birthday?
- Where is your desk?
- Is your notebook new?

- Who is our teacher?
- Why do you like school?
- Are you from Mexico?

> **Grammar Check ✔**
>
> Name some contractions.

10

Writing

Describe a Person

When you describe a person, you can say what the person looks like, or you can focus on the person's actions.

Writing Prompt

Write a paragraph describing a person. Tell about the person's actions. Say what these actions show about the person. Be sure to use be verbs correctly.

① Prewrite

Choose a person to write about. Think about this person's actions. What do the person's actions tell you about him or her? List your ideas in a T-Chart.

A student named Maria listed her ideas like this:

MY MOTHER	
HER ACTIONS	**WHAT HER ACTIONS SHOW**
smiles a lot	friendly
visits our neighbor	kind
spends time with me	patient and loving

② Draft

Use your T-Chart to help you write a first draft.
- Keep in mind your purpose—to describe a person.
- Tell what the person's actions show about him or her.

③ Revise

Reread your draft. Look for places where it needs improvement. Use the Writing Checklist to help you find problems. Then revise your draft.

④ Edit

Check your work for errors. Use the Peer Review Checklist on page 402.

⑤ Publish

Make a clean copy of your final draft. Share it with the class. Save your work. You will need it for the Writing Workshop.

Here is Maria's description:

Maria Gonzalez

My mother is friendly. She says hi to people and smiles at them. Our neighbor, Mrs. King, lives alone. My mother visits her every afternoon. Mrs. King says my mother is the kindest woman she knows. My mother spends a lot of time with me. She and I talk a lot. She is very patient and loving. She's a great mom!

WB
11–12

What You Will Learn

Reading
- Vocabulary building: *Context, phonics*
- Reading strategy: *Preview*
- Text type: *Literature (short story)*

Grammar
Simple present

Writing
Describe a typical summer day

These words will help you understand the reading.

Key Words

dessert

friend

fold

mix

Key Words

Making Friends is a story about two new children in a school.

Words in Context

1 Which dessert would you like to eat?

2 Meg likes to run with her friend, Tom. What do you like to do with a friend?

3 Myra likes to <mark>fold</mark> paper.
She makes paper birds.

4 Juan can <mark>mix</mark> things.
He helps his grandfather cook.

Practice

Make flashcards to help you memorize the words.

- Write a key word on the front.
- On the back, write the meaning.

Make Connections

Families may visit a new place. Do you remember a time when you were in a new place? Describe how you felt. Use some of the key words as you speak.

WB
13

These words will help you talk about the reading.

Academic Words

create
make something

task
job that must be done

Academic Words

Words in Context

Our art teacher shows us how to **create** fun things.

When it is time to clean up, our teacher gives everyone a **task**. I have to put away the books.

Practice

Complete each sentence. Use an academic word.

1. My mother can _____ beautiful pictures on the computer.

2. Tomorrow we are going to do a group project. My _____ is to bring a newspaper to school.

Apply

Write the answers in your notebook. Use the academic words. Then ask and answer with a partner.

1. What do you like to do in your free time? Do you like to **create** or make things like Myra on page 23? What do you **create**?

2. What **tasks** at home or at school do you enjoy? What **tasks** don't you enjoy?

Phonics

Long Vowels with Silent e

Each vowel can stand for more than one sound.
Listen. Then read each word aloud.

a		i		o		u	
hat	hate	hid	hide	hop	hope	hug	huge
can	cane	lick	like	not	note	cub	cube

- The words in the gray boxes have short vowels.
- The words in the white boxes have long vowels.
- Listen again. Which vowels sound like their own names?

Rule

The vowel is long when it is followed by a consonant and the letter e. The letter e is silent.

Short Vowel	Long Vowel
m a d	m a d e
C V C	C V C e

Practice

Work with a partner. Take turns.

- Circle the words with a long vowel sound.
  tube   cone   sit   back   bake   tub   con   site
- Read the words to a partner.

Literature
Short Story

🎧 **Listen to the Audio.**
Listen for the general meaning. Use the pictures to help you understand the selection.

Reading Strategy

Preview

To preview means to look at the pages before you read.

- Read the title.
- Look at the illustrations.
- Try to predict what the text is about.

Listen as your teacher models the reading strategy.

Making Friends

by Dan Ahearn
illustrated by Laurie Keller

The girls and boys in Miss Jones's class are from many **different** countries. But every family does fun things. Girls and boys can teach these fun things to friends .

Kate teaches a song to Juan. Juan tells a story to Kate. Maria shows Ben how to play a game. Most of the girls and boys are smiling. They are having fun.

But Hana and Carlos are sad.

---

different   not like something or someone else

Before You Go On

What fun things do the girls and boys in the story teach each other?

Hana just came to this school. She is from **Japan**. Hana does not have a friend yet.

Carlos just came here. He is from Mexico. Carlos does not have a friend yet.

Miss Jones tells Carlos to sit by Hana. She asks Hana to teach a fun thing to Carlos. Hana says she can make paper animals. Her mother showed her how. Carlos thinks that is a fun thing to do.

Japan   country in Asia

Hana takes out some paper. She makes a paper crane. A crane is a bird. Carlos asks Hana to show him how to make a paper crane. Hana shows him how to <mark>fold</mark> the paper. Carlos makes a paper crane, too.

Now what can Carlos do? Carlos can make a <mark>dessert</mark>. But he needs his mother to help. He will teach Hana how to make a dessert.

Before You Go On

What special item does Hana create?

Hana goes to Carlos's house. His mother gives Carlos the things he needs. He **mixes** them. Carlos shows Hana how to make the dessert. Hana mixes the things, too.

His mother cooks the dessert. Carlos and Hana watch. It is fun making dessert! Soon, the dessert is ready. Hana tastes the dessert. It is so good!

At school, they will show other girls and boys what they learned.

Reading Skill

The word **show** is a basic sight word. Sight words are words you see a lot when you read.

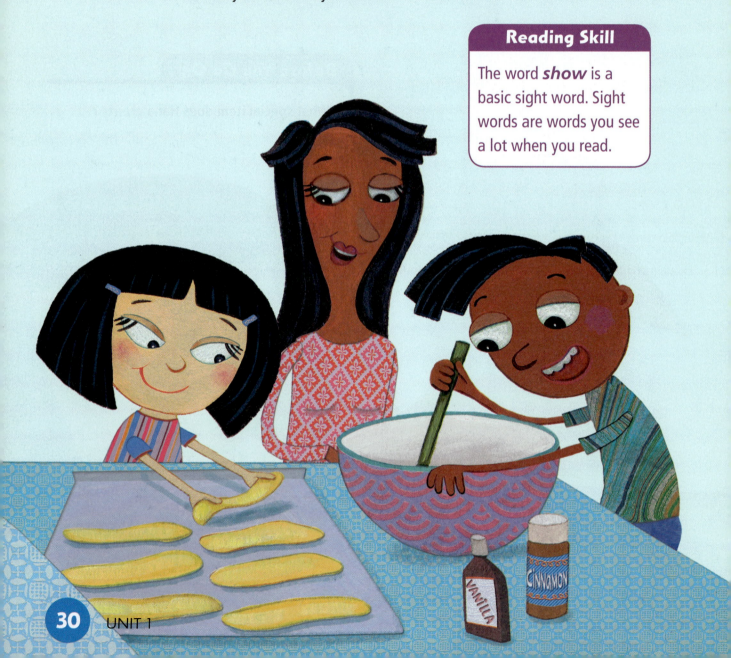

Hana shows the dessert they made. Carlos showed her how to make the dessert.

Carlos shows a paper crane he made. Hana showed him how to make the paper crane.

The other girls and boys taste the dessert. They make paper cranes. Carlos and Hana show them how.

Hana and Carlos can do new things. All of the girls and boys can do new things, too. Hana and Carlos now have many friends.

16–18

Think It Over

1. **Recall** What **task** does the teacher give Hana?

2. **Comprehend** What do Hana and Carlos have in common?

3. **Analyze** Why are Hana and Carlos happy at the end of the story?

Reading Strategy

Preview

- Did previewing help you predict what the story would be about?

- How else did previewing help you understand the story?

Learning Strategies

Sequence of Events

Events are things that happen in a story. Events happen in a certain order. This order is called the **sequence**.

Practice

Read these events from *Making Friends*. Number the events 1–6 in the order that they happen in the story.

☐ Carlos and Hana are sad.

☐ Carlos shows Hana how to make a <mark>dessert</mark>.

☐ Carlos and Hana share what they learned with the other girls and boys.

☐ Carlos and Hana watch Carlos's mother cook the dessert.

☐ Hana shows Carlos how to make a paper bird.

☐ Hana goes to Carlos's house.

Use a Sequence Chart

A Sequence Chart can help you think about events in the order that they happen.

Practice GO 4

Copy the chart. Answer the questions.

1.	2.	3.	4.
Hana and Carlos don't have **friends**.	Hana shows Carlos how to make a paper bird.		Hana and Carlos share what they learned with the other girls and boys.

5.

1. Which event should be in box 3?
   a. Hana and Carlos are sad.
   b. Hana shows Carlos how to make a dessert.
   c. Hana and Carlos have fun with their new friends.
   d. Carlos shows Hana how to make a dessert.

2. Choose an event to add to the last box.
   a. Hana and Carlos are sad.
   b. Hana and Carlos become friends with the other girls and boys.
   c. Carlos's mother cooks the dessert.
   d. Carlos needs his mother's help.

19

Apply

Retell the story to a partner. Use some of the key words as you speak.

Extension

Think of something you know how to make. Teach a partner how to make it. Then switch roles and follow your partner's directions.

Grammar

Simple Present

Verbs in the simple present tell what usually happens. They change form to agree with the subject of the sentence.

If the subject is *he*, *she*, or *it*, add *-s* or *-es* to the verb.

Subject	Verb	Verb	Verb
I/You/We/They	**fold**	**stop**	**mix**
He/She/It	**folds**	**stops**	**mixes**

To make **negative sentences**, add *do not* or *does not* before the base form of the verb.

Affirmative   **Negative**
She **smiles**. → She **does not smile.**

do not → don't
does not → doesn't

To make **questions**, use *do* or *does* before the subject.

Does Carlos **help** his mother?
Yes, he **does**.

Do you **watch** sports?
No, I **don't**.

Practice A

Circle the correct form of the verb.

1. Carlos (mix / (mixes)) things. *Carlos mixes things.*

2. The teacher (ask / asks) questions.

3. I (fold / folds) the paper in half.

4. Her **friend** (smile / smiles).

5. My **friends** (like / likes) dessert.

Practice B

Rewrite the sentences from Practice A in your notebook.
Make them negative.

Apply

Work with a partner. Ask and answer the questions.
Use the simple present in your answers.

Example: A: Do you walk to school?

B: Yes, I walk to school.

- Do you walk to school?
- Do your friends live near you?
- Does your father fix things?
- Do you like cold weather?
- Does your mother watch television?
- Do you help at home?
- Does your teacher smile a lot?
- Do you like dessert?

> **Grammar Check ✔**
> Make a sentence using the **simple present**.

Writing

Describe a Sunny Day

When you describe an event, you tell who is there
and what they do.

Writing Prompt

Write a paragraph describing a typical sunny day. Tell about who you
are with and what you do. Be sure to use the simple present correctly.

① **Prewrite**

Choose a typical sunny day to write about. Who are you with?
What things do you do? List your ideas in a graphic organizer.

A student named Anthea listed her ideas like this:

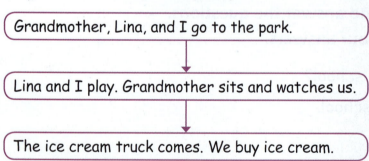

My Sunny Days

Grandmother, Lina, and I go to the park.

Lina and I play. Grandmother sits and watches us.

The ice cream truck comes. We buy ice cream.

② **Draft**

Use your graphic organizer to help you write a first draft.

• Keep in mind your purpose—to describe.
• Include details about people and actions.

Revise

Reread your draft. Look for places where it needs improvement. Use the Writing Checklist to help you find problems. Then revise your draft.

Edit

Check your work for errors. Use the Peer Review Checklist on page 402.

⑤ Publish

Make a clean copy of your final draft. Share it with the class. Save your work. You will need it for the Writing Workshop.

Here is Anthea's description:

> **Writing Checklist**
>
> ✓ **Ideas**
> I included interesting details.
> I expressed my ideas clearly.
>
> ✓ **Conventions**
> I used verbs in the simple present correctly.
> Subjects and verbs agree.

Anthea Najjar

During summer vacation I go to the park near my apartment. My sister, Lina, and I play. Our grandmother sits on a bench and watches us. Later, the ice cream truck arrives. Lina and I race to be first. I ask for chocolate. Lina's favorite is strawberry. As we walk home, I smell flowers and grass. I love these sunny days.

21–22

What You Will Learn

Reading

- Vocabulary building: *Context, word study*
- Reading strategy: *Make connections*
- Text type: *Literature (personal narrative)*

Grammar

Nouns: singular and plural

Writing

Describe a family celebration

These words will help you understand the reading.

Key Words

celebrate

crowd

company

weekend

gathers

Key Words

In *My Family*, a girl describes her family. She tells what her family does together.

Words in Context

1 I like to **celebrate** my birthday. It makes me feel special.

2 Many children are in one place. These children make a **crowd**.

3 We like to have **company** for dinner.

4 The <mark>weekend</mark> is Saturday and Sunday. We do not have school. We work in the community garden.

5 All the family <mark>gathers</mark> around to hear Grandmother sing.

Make flash cards to help you memorize the words.
- Write a word on the front.
- On the back, write a sentence. But leave a blank where the key word should be.

Make Connections

In the story *My Family*, a girl tells what she likes to do with her family. Describe what you like to do with your family. Use some of the key words as you speak.

23

These words will help you talk about the reading.

Academic Words

contribute
give something

similar
almost the same, but not quite

Academic Words

Words in Context

My family likes to **contribute** old books to the town library.

Every month, the lunch menu at our school is **similar** to the month before.

Practice

Use an academic word to complete each sentence.

1. Everyone in the class has to _____ something to the party. I'm going to bring juice.

2. Pink is _____ to the color red, but pink is lighter.

Apply

Write the answers in your notebook. Use the academic words. Then ask and answer with a partner.

1. When it is time to clean up the classroom, how do you **contribute**?

2. How are you **similar** to a family member or another important person in your life?

W B
24

Word Study

Use a Dictionary

Read this dictionary entry.

> **gath • er** (gathər) verb **1** to bring or come together <gather your things>. **2** to gain little by little <gather speed>. **3** to come to a conclusion <gather that you are going>.
> **gathered, gathering**.

Practice

Work with a partner.

- The entry for **gather** has more than one meaning.
- Find the meaning that makes sense in each sentence.

    1. Anna started to **gather** speed on her bike.

    2. Gather your books together.

    3. I **gather** that this reading is about a family.

Literature
Personal Narrative

More About THE BiG QUESTION

How is your family
a community?

🎧 **Listen to the Audio.**
Listen for the general meaning.
Use the pictures to help you
understand the selection.

Reading Strategy
Make Connections

As you read, think about your
family.

- What does your family
  celebrate?
- Who comes when you
  celebrate?
- What special things do you do?

Listen as your teacher models the
reading strategy.

My Family

by Hanna Jamal
illustrated by Kathryn Mitter

My family likes to celebrate. We like
to be together.

Monday through Friday, everyone is
busy. We go to school. We go to work.
We do homework. We do **chores**.

But on the weekend, we get
together. And whenever my family gets
together, we always have a good time.

---

chores   jobs that you have to do often

I live in Madison, Wisconsin, with my parents and my brother. My grandparents live in Madison, too. My aunts and uncles live in Milwaukee, Wisconsin. On some weekends, we drive to Milwaukee to visit them. On other weekends, they drive to Madison to visit us.

I like it when we get together. We talk, laugh, and play games. There is **plenty** of food to eat. There is plenty of noise! You can tell that everyone is happy to be together.

---

plenty a lot

Before You Go On

When does the family get together?

READING 3 **43**

Sometimes, we celebrate a special day. Today we celebrate my grandmother's birthday. We all work together to plan her party.

My mother bakes a cake, and my cousins and I put up **streamers**. We each have a gift to give to my grandmother.

We sing the birthday song. My grandfather smiles. He sings, too.

---

streamers long, thin colored paper

There are a lot of **candles** on my grandmother's cake! We watch her blow out the candles. We ask her what she wished for, but she will not say.

My grandmother has fun at her birthday party. She is happy to have the family together.

I think I know what she wished for. Her wish is to have many more family celebrations .

---

candles   sticks of wax that burn and give light

Before You Go On

How does the family show their love for the grandmother?

When the weather is warm, friends join our family celebrations. Company gathers in our yard. Neighbors, friends, and family come over. There is a big crowd.

Everyone brings something to the party. There is plenty of food. Dad cooks. Mom makes **salad**. We drink **lemonade**. We eat dessert.

We laugh and talk. We play games and have fun. You can tell that we are having a good time. I like to see everyone together.

---

salad   a dish of raw leafy vegetables

lemonade   a sweet drink made from lemon juice

At last, the party is over. The neighbors go home. Our friends go home, too. The aunts, uncles, and cousins say goodbye. My grandmother and grandfather say good night.

Now it is quiet. But next weekend, we will have another celebration. We will see the whole family together again.

26–28

Reading Strategy

Make Connections

- How is your family **similar** to the one in the story?

- How is your family different from the one in the story?

- How did making connections help you understand the story?

Think It Over

1. **Recall** Where does the family have celebrations?

2. **Comprehend** How do friends and family members **contribute** to the parties?

3. **Analyze** How do friends and family members feel about each other? Give examples.

A Family Tree

Grandmother ▶
She is my
mother's mother.

◀ **Grandfather**
He is my
mother's father.

▲ **Aunt**
She is my uncle's wife.

▲ **Uncle**
He is my mother's brother.

▲ **Mother**
This is my mother.

Amelia ▶
Hi! I'm Amelia. This
is my family tree.

▲ **Cousin**
He is my aunt and uncle's son.

Grandmother ▶
She is my
father's mother.

◀ **Grandfather**
He is my
father's father.

◀ **Father**
This is my father.

▲ **Brother**
This is my brother.

▲ **Sister**
This is my sister.

Activity to Do

These two pages use words
and pictures to tell you about
family trees.

- Think about your family.
- Make a family tree using
  pictures and words.
- Post your family tree in
  your classroom.

Learning Strategies

Make Connections

Your family may be like another family. It may be different. You can ask yourself questions to learn about families.

- How are my family <mark>celebrations</mark> **similar** to the celebrations in the story?
- How are my family celebrations different from the celebrations in the story?

Practice

Look back at the story. Answer the questions.

1. What do the aunts and uncles do at family celebrations?
2. How does the family <mark>celebrate</mark> the grandmother's birthday?
3. What does the family do when <mark>company</mark> comes over?

Use a T-Chart

You can use a T-chart to show how things are alike and different.

Practice GO 9

Answer the questions below. Tell about the family in the story. Tell about your own family.

Story Family	Your Family
1. They get together on the weekend.	1.
2. Her aunts, uncles, cousins . . .	2.
3.	3.
4.	4.

1. When do you get together?
2. Who comes to the celebrations?
3. What do different family members do?
4. What do you do with family and friends?

Apply

Summarize the story for a partner.

W B
29

Extension

Think of a special thing you do with your family. Describe this to a partner. Tell who is there. Tell what you do.

Grammar

Nouns: Singular and Plural

A **singular noun** names one person, place, or thing.
A **plural noun** names two or more people, places, or things.

most nouns, add *-s*	crowd → crowd**s**
nouns ending in *-s, -ch, -sh,* or *-x,* add *-es*	dress → dress**es** wish → wish**es**
nouns ending in vowel + consonant + *-y*, change *-y* to *-i* and add *-es*	family → famil**ies** baby → bab**ies**
irregular nouns, **look them up in the dictionary**	child → **children** person → **people**

Use *the* to refer to something specific.

Let's sing **the** birthday song.

Use *a* before singular, countable nouns that begin with consonants. Use *an* before singular, countable nouns that begin with vowels.

I have **a** banana. My sister has **an** orange.

Use *this* or *that* with singular nouns; *these* or *those* with plural nouns.

This cake is delicious. **That** cake is old.
These cakes are delicious. **Those** cakes are old.

Practice A

Complete the sentences with the plural form.

1. I see many _____people_____ in the park.
   (person)

2. We have two _____ this week.
   (party)

3. Look at all the _____! (box)

4. You have three _____ to play. (hour)

Practice B

Circle the correct answer.

1. Did you make (this / these) cookies?

2. (That / Those) computer costs a lot of money.

3. Manny dropped (the / those) fragile vase.

Apply

Work with a partner. Ask and answer the questions. Use singular and plural nouns in your answers.

Example: A: How many pencils do you have?

B: I have two pencils.

- How many pencils do you have?
- What do you have in your backpack?
- What do you have in your room at home?

Writing

Describe a Family Celebration

There are many ways to describe events. One way is to describe everything you remember about a special event.

① Prewrite GO 13

Choose a family celebration to write about. Who is there? What does everyone do to prepare? List your ideas in a word web.

A student named Hideo listed his ideas like this:

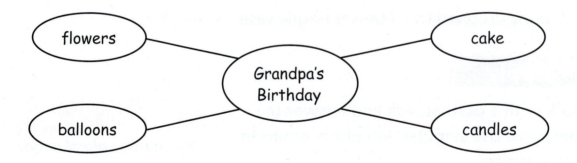

② Draft

Use your word web to help you write a first draft.
- Keep in mind your purpose—to describe.
- Include details about the people and what they do.

③ Revise

Reread your draft. Look for places where it needs improvement. Use the Writing Checklist to help you find problems. Then revise your draft.

④ Edit

Check your work for errors. Use the Peer Review Checklist on page 402.

⑤ Publish

Make a clean copy of your final draft. Share it with the class. Save your work. You will need it for the Writing Workshop.

Here is Hideo's description of a family celebration:

Writing Checklist

✓ **Ideas**
I included interesting details.
I expressed my ideas clearly.

✓ **Conventions**
I used verbs in the present tense correctly.

Hideo Furuya

Every year, we have a birthday party for my grandfather. The whole family works together. My cousins put flowers around the house. My aunts make a beautiful cake. My sisters put candles on the cake. My brothers put up balloons in the living room. Then we hide. We hear my grandfather's feet on the front porch. When he opens the door, we yell, "Surprise!"

31–32

Apply and Extend

Link the Readings

Read the words in the top row.

- For *Lin's Shopping Day*, put an X under the words that remind you of the selection.

- Repeat the same activity for the other readings.

	Informational text	Literature	Being nice to neighbors	Planning a party
Lin's Shopping Day				
Making Friends				
My Family				

Discussion

1. How are Lin and Hana **similar**?

2. In the story *Making Friends*, how do Carlos and Hana get to know their classmates?

3. In the story *My Family*, how do the family members and friends **contribute** to the celebrations?

 THE BiG QUESTION What are some ways that communities are alike and different?

> **Listening Skills**
>
> Take notes as you listen. Use your notes to ask questions.

Projects

Your teacher will help you choose one of these projects.

Written	Oral	Visual/Active
Lists List three things you like about your community and three things that you wish you could change.	**Conversation** Talk with someone who moved from one community to another. How are the places alike and different?	**Postcards** Make a postcard that shows the community in *Lin's Shopping Day*. Make a postcard that shows your community.
Letters Write letters between you and a character in one of the stories. Tell each other about your communities.	**Town Song** Write new words to *The Wheels on the Bus* to create the song *The People in Our Town*. Teach others to sing it.	**Comic Strip** Find out about a community in another country. Create a comic strip that shows what children do there.

W B
33–34

Listening and Speaking Workshop
Play a Description Guessing Game

You are going to describe a place in the community. Then you will listen as your classmates talk about a place in the community.

① Prepare

A. Choose a place in your community. You will describe this place, but you won't name it. Your classmates will guess the place.

B. Close your eyes. Visualize the place you are going to describe. Write down some details.

> **Useful Language**
>
> 🎧 Listen and Repeat.
>
> This place is [quiet / busy].
>
> This place is in [the city center / country].
>
> There are many [people / animals / books].
>
> I like this place because . . .

> This place is in the city. There are many animals in this place. The animals are not pets like dogs or cats. I go to this place on the weekend with my family. I usually visit the area with the pandas. What is the name of this place?

② Practice

Practice your presentation five times or more. Practice in front of your family or friends. If possible, record your presentation. Then listen to yourself. How do you sound? Record yourself again and try to improve.

③ **Present**

As you speak, do the following:

- Don't be nervous. Have fun.

- Describe a place in the community. Ask your classmates to guess what place you are describing.

As you listen, do the following:

- Listen quietly to your classmates. Don't call out any guesses. Wait until your classmates ask for them.

- If you don't understand something a speaker says, you can say, "Excuse me. Could you repeat that, please?"

④ **Evaluate**

After you speak, answer these questions:

✔ Did you understand the game rules?

✔ Did you choose good description words?

After you listen, answer these questions:

✔ Did you understand the speaker?

✔ Did you guess the place?

Writing Workshop

Describe an Event

Writing Prompt

Write an essay describing an event. Describe what happened in the order that it happened. Include specific words and vivid details.

① Prewrite

Review the writing you have done for this unit. Now choose a topic. Think of an event that was interesting. List the details of the event in a graphic organizer.

A student named Zhang Wei listed his ideas like this:

> I want to do something special for Mom's birthday.

> Dad and I make her breakfast.

> Mom is really surprised.

② Draft

Use your graphic organizer to write a first draft.

- Keep in mind your purpose—to describe an event.
- Include details that help the reader create a mental picture.

③ Revise

Read your draft. Look for places where the writing needs improvement. Use the Writing Checklist to help you find problems. Then revise your draft.

Six Traits of Writing Checklist

 Ideas
Are all of my sentences related to the topic?

 Organization
Are my ideas in the right order?

 Voice
Is my writing lively?

 Word Choice
Do my words create pictures in the reader's mind?

 Sentence Fluency
Did I use different kinds of sentences?

 Conventions
Are my verbs in the correct tense?

Here is how Zhang Wei revised his essay:

Zhang Wei

The Breakfast Surprise

Every weekend Mom makes a special breakfast. Sometimes I help. It's our special time together. To surprise her on her birthday, I make breakfast for her. Dad helps. We decide to make pancake^s.

Revised to correct plural form.

First, I look up the recipe in Mom's cookbook. It says to melt butter. We melt the butter and mix it with eggs and milk. Next, we stir the flour together with other dry ingredients. Dad stirs too hard, and the flour mixture goes all over his face and clothes. He looks funny. We laugh.

After we cook~~s~~ the pancakes, I call Mom to the kitchen. She is so surprised! Then she sees the flour all over Dad and laughs, too.

Revised to correct verb agreement.

④ Edit

Check your work for errors. Trade papers with a partner. Use the Peer Review Checklist.

⑤ Publish

Make a clean copy of your final draft.
Share it with the class.

35–36

Peer Review Checklist

✔ The details of the event are in order.

✔ The writing is interesting.

✔ Pronouns and verbs agree.

Spelling Tip

Add -es to 3rd person singular verbs in the simple present if the verb ends in -s, -ch, -sh, or -x. If the verb ends in y, change y to i, then add -es.

Fluency

Listen to the sentences. Pay attention to the groups of words. Read aloud.

1. Lin likes to visit many places in her community.

2. New friends can teach each other new things.

3. Many families like to celebrate special days together.

Work in pairs. Take turns reading the passage below aloud for one minute. Count the number of words you read.

Making Friends tells about a classroom of children from all	10
over the world. The teacher wants them to teach each other	21
something fun. Hana is from Japan and Carlos is from Mexico.	32
They are sad because they don't know anyone yet.	41
In class, Hana shows Carlos how to make a bird from paper.	53
Carlos folds paper and makes a crane. Carlos wants to show	64
Hana how to make a dessert at his house. Hana and Carlos make	77
a good dessert.	80

With your partner, find the words that slowed you down.

- Practice saying each word and then say the sentence each word is in.

- Then take turns reading the text again. Count the number of words you read.

W|B
37

Taking Tests

You will often take tests that help show what you know. Follow these tips to improve your test-taking skills.

Coaching Corner

Answering Test Questions

- Sometimes you will answer test questions that are based on reading selections. At other times, you will use a picture or a chart to help you answer a question.

- Before you answer a question based on a picture, read the question carefully. Be sure you understand what the question is asking. Study the picture closely before you choose an answer.

- When questions are based on a reading selection, first read the selection, then read the questions. After you choose an answer, review the reading passage again to make sure your answer is correct.

Read and answer the question below.

1 This is a _____.

    A turtle

    B clock

    C flower

    D baseball

Tip
✔ Study the picture to find the answer.

Read the selection. Then answer the questions.

Station #39

    Each year our class takes a field trip to visit the fire station. We all climb inside the fire truck and explore. Rick pretends to turn on the siren. Jesse tries on a firefighter's hat. Rosa plays with the fire station's dog. Chris slides down the fire pole. Then, the fire chief tells us about fire safety. We always enjoy our visit to the fire station!

2 Who is Jesse?

    A the fire chief

    B a dog

    C the author

    D a student in the class

3 In the first sentence, the word <u>takes</u> means —

    F goes on

    G plans

    H grabs

    J walks to

Tips
✔ To answer Question 2, look for the people doing the action in most of the sentences.
✔ Think about the meaning of each of the answer choices. Which one makes sense?

Build Unit Vocabulary

What do you know about meeting challenges?

Words to Know

Listen and repeat. Use these words to talk about meeting challenges.

| practice | study | rehearse | train |

Practice

Work with a partner. Look up these words in a dictionary.
Then ask and answer questions.

| a race | a test | a school play | a piano lesson |

Example: A: What are you <u>training</u> for?

B: I'm <u>training</u> for <u>a race</u>.

Write

Read the question. Write your response in your notebook.

What is something you practice, train, rehearse, or study for?
Write two or three sentences about it.

Make Connections

Copy the sentences into your notebook and complete them.

perform before an audience

get good grades

win or get a medal

act in a play

1. I like to run. I train after school every day.

I want to _____ in a race this year.

2. I'm in the school play this year. It's my first time

to _____. It's fun!

3. I practice the piano every day. Soon I can

_____!

4. I ask a lot of questions in class, so I learn a lot.

I study hard, too, so I usually _____.

What about you?

Talk with a partner about some of the challenges you have at school and at home. How do you meet these challenges? Who can help you?

Costa Rica

Pedro

In Costa Rica, we have many rain forests. Our rain forests are in danger. Some people want to cut down the trees. Then the animals will not have homes. My parents and I try to help. We teach people about the animals in the rain forest.

Abebe

I live in Ethiopia. I want to be a good runner. Each morning, I train before I go to school. Each afternoon, I train after school. Then I go home and do my homework. If I train hard, I can be a great runner.

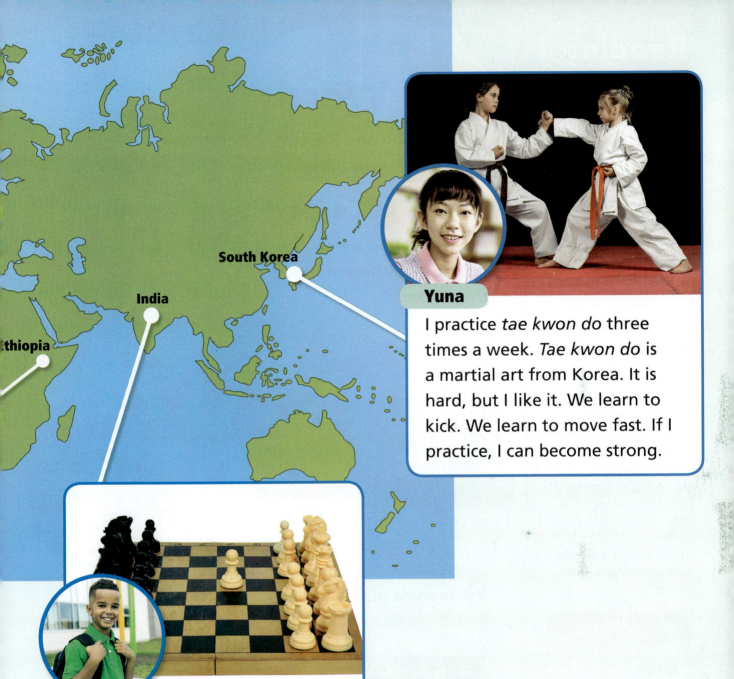

South Korea

India

Ethiopia

Yuna

I practice *tae kwon do* three times a week. *Tae kwon do* is a martial art from Korea. It is hard, but I like it. We learn to kick. We learn to move fast. If I practice, I can become strong.

Krishna

I live in India. Every day after school, I do my homework. Then I go to see my chess coach. I play chess with her for two hours. If I work hard, I can enter a chess contest.

What about you?

1. What do you challenge yourself to do, either every day or a few times a week?

2. How did you meet a big challenge in your life? Share your story.

What You Will Learn

Reading
- Vocabulary building: *Context, phonics*
- Reading strategy: *Identify events in a plot*
- Text type: *Literature (play)*

Grammar
Possessive nouns and pronouns

Writing
Write a plot summary

These words will help you understand the reading.

Key Words

dinner

well

roars

reflection

Key Words

In *The Rabbit and the Lion*, a smart rabbit plays a trick on a proud lion.

Words in Context

1 All around the world, people eat different foods for **dinner**.

2 In some places, people get water from a **well**. A **well** is a deep hole in the ground.

3 Different animals make different noises. A duck quacks. A horse neighs. A lion ==roars==!

4 The ==reflection== in this lake is very clear. You can see the mountains, trees, and clouds in the water.

Practice

Make flashcards to help you memorize the words.

- Write a key word on the front.
- On the back, draw a picture of the word.

Make Connections

What is your favorite animal?
Why is it your favorite? Discuss.

Speaking Skills

If you don't know the exact English word to use, explain your idea with words you know.

41

These words will help you talk about the reading.

Academic Words

focus
pay attention to

identify
tell what something is

Academic Words

Words in Context

When I take a test, I **focus** on the easy questions first.

My dad can **identify** different kinds of airplanes by their shape.

Practice

Choose an academic word to complete each sentence. Write your answers in the blank.

1. I can _____ different kinds of birds by the colors of their feathers.

2. Hanna can't watch TV now. She has to _____ on her homework.

Apply

Ask and answer with a partner.

1. Can you **focus** on your homework and listen to music at the same time?

2. How can you **identify** something that is cooking in the kitchen before you see it?

Phonics

Long Vowel Pairs

Long vowel sounds can be spelled with two vowels together making a pair. Listen. Then read each word aloud.

Long *o* Pairs		Long *u* Pairs	
road	foe	blue	fruit

Rule

When two vowels are together, the first vowel says its name.
- The letters *oa* or *oe* usually have the long *o* sound.
- The letters *ue* or *ui* usually have the long *u* sound.

Practice

Work with a partner. Take turns sounding out the words in the box.

clue	toad	woe	foam	fruit	suit
doe	true	loan	toe	cue	soak

- List the words from the box that have the long o sound.
- List the words from the box that have the long u sound.

43

Literature
Play

More About THE BiG QUESTION

Sometimes, a character meets a challenge with quick thinking. How can thinking be helpful?

Listen to the Audio.

Listen for the general meaning. Use the pictures to help you understand the selection.

Reading Strategy

Identify Events in a Plot

As you read, think about the important events.

- Lion catches Rabbit.
- Rabbit tries to save himself. How?

Listen as your teacher models the reading strategy.

The Rabbit and the Lion

by Ed Vuong
illustrated by Tim Haggerty

Characters
Narrator
Rabbit
Lion

---

characters   people or animals in a play or story
narrator   person who tells a story

Narrator: Rabbit is smart. But one night his **foe**, Lion, catches him.

Rabbit: Help!

Lion: I have you now, Rabbit! I am going to eat you for dinner!

Rabbit: I am too small. You need a big animal to eat.

Lion: Yes. But you are just the right size for a **snack**.

Rabbit: Who are you to go around eating rabbits?

Lion: I am king of this forest!

Rabbit: Look at the lion in the well. He says he is king!

---

foe enemy

snack small bit of food to eat

Before You Go On

How does Rabbit change Lion's **focus** so he is thinking about himself and not about Rabbit?

Narrator:	Lion looks into the well. He sees a lion in the water.
Rabbit:	Ha! Ha! He thinks his own reflection is another lion!
Narrator:	Lion roars at his own reflection in the water in the well.
Lion:	You are a **fake**! I AM KING OF THIS FOREST!
Narrator:	But a strange voice comes back out of the well.
Voice:	I AM KING OF THIS FOREST!
Rabbit:	Hee! Hee! It is this silly king's own voice. It is an **echo**.

---

fake   someone who is not what they seem to be

echo   sound you hear again

Reading Skill

Ask your classmates or your teacher if you do not understand a word, phrase, or language structure.

Lion:	Fake! You will be sorry for this!
Narrator:	Lion jumps into the well. But the other lion is gone!
Lion:	Where are you? Come out!
Rabbit:	I guess I am king of this forest tonight. See you tomorrow, Lion.

44–46

Reading Strategy

Identify Events in a Plot

- What does Rabbit tell Lion?
- What does Lion do?
- How did **identifying** the events help you see how Rabbit saves himself?

Think It Over

1. **Recall** What does Lion want to do to Rabbit?

2. **Comprehend** Lion cannot **identify** himself in his reflection. Who does he think is in the well?

3. **Analyze** What happens when Lion roars into the well? Why does this make him more angry?

Learning Strategies

Events in a Plot

Events are the things that happen in a play. The events make up the plot. The **plot** is the main story of a play.

Practice

Read these lines from the play. Tell who says each line. Then tell which events show how Rabbit tricks Lion.

1. Help!
2. But you are just the right size for a snack.
3. I am king of this forest!
4. Look at the lion in the well. He says he is king!
5. Ha! Ha! He thinks his own reflection is another lion!
6. Lion jumps into the well.

Use a Sequence Chart

In this play, the events happen in a certain order. One event makes the next one happen.

Practice

GO 4

Answer the questions. Write your answers in the Sequence Chart.

1. Which is the best sentence for Number 3 in the chart?
   a. Lion jumps into the well.
   b. Rabbit thinks the reflection in the well is another lion.
   c. Lion thinks his reflection in the well is another lion.

2. Which is the best sentence for Number 6 in the chart?
   a. Lion jumps into the well to fight his reflection.
   b. Rabbit says that Lion is king of this forest.
   c. Lion says that Rabbit is king of this forest.

1	Lion catches Rabbit. Lion says that he is going to eat Rabbit.
2	Rabbit says there is another lion in the well.
3	
4	Lion ==roars== and shouts at the reflection in the well.
5	An echo from the well comes back out at Lion.
6	

W B
47

Apply

Retell the play to a partner.
Refer to the pictures as you speak.

Extension

Write a shorter version of the play that shows how the characters solved a problem. Present your skit to the class.

Grammar

Pronouns and Possessives

A **pronoun** takes the place of a noun. Here are two types of personal pronouns.

Subject Pronouns		Object Pronouns	
I	it	me	it
you	we	you	us
he/she	they	him/her	them

A pronoun must match the noun it replaces in gender and number. The replaced noun is called the **antecedent.**

Mario is hungry. **He** wants <mark>dinner</mark>.   **Mario and Ana** like **sushi**. **They** eat **it** a lot.

Possessives

Use **possessive pronouns** or **possessive nouns** to show ownership. For plural nouns ending in -s, just add an apostrophe.

Possessive Pronouns		Possessive Nouns
mine	its	the **lion's** reflection
yours	ours	the **king's** voice
his	theirs	the **students'** questions
hers		

Whose

To ask a question about possession, use *whose.*

Whose pencil is this? ⟶ It's mine.

Practice A

Write the pronouns for each noun.

Object Pronoun	Possessive Pronoun
1. George _him_	_____
2. my friends _____	_____
3. my parents and I _____	_____
4. Isabel _____	_____

Practice B

Change the underlined nouns into pronouns.
Write the sentences in your notebook.

1. <u>This book</u> is interesting. _It is interesting_.

2. Karen invited <u>Jade and me</u> to her party.

3. <u>The students</u> have a new teacher.

4. <u>Ana and I</u> like fairy tales.

5. <u>Bruce</u> is my brother.

Apply

Work with a partner. Ask and answer the questions.
Use possessive nouns and pronouns in your answers.

Example: A: Whose pen is this?   B: It's mine.

- Whose books are those?
- Whose backpack is that?
- Whose eraser is that?
- Whose desk is that over there?
- Whose picture is that on the wall?

W B
48

Grammar Check ✔

Name some **possessive pronouns**.

Writing
Write a Plot Summary

One way to write about a story is to summarize the plot. This means you tell the main ideas in the story.

Writing Prompt

Write a paragraph summarizing the plot of a story. Tell the events in the correct order. Include details about what the characters say and do. Be sure to use possessive nouns and pronouns correctly.

① Prewrite

Choose a story to summarize. Who are the characters? What are the events that happen? List your ideas in a Sequence Chart.

A student named Bruno listed his ideas like this:

THE RABBIT AND THE LION

Lion catches Rabbit. He wants to eat Rabbit.

↓

Rabbit tricks Lion. Lion thinks there is another lion in the well.

↓

Lion jumps into the well. Rabbit is safe.

② Draft

Use your Sequence Chart to help you write a first draft.

- Keep in mind your purpose—to write a plot summary.
- Include the events of the story in the correct order.

③ Revise

Reread your draft. Look for places where it needs improvement. Use the Writing Checklist to help you find problems. Then revise your draft.

④ Edit

Check your work for errors. Use the Peer Review Checklist on page 402.

⑤ Publish

Make a clean copy of your final draft. Share it with the class. Save your work. You will need it for the Writing Workshop.

Here is Bruno's plot summary:

Writing Checklist

✔ **Ideas**
I included all the events in the correct order.

I expressed my ideas clearly.

✔ **Conventions**
I used pronouns correctly.

I used possessive nouns ('s) correctly.

Bruno Silva

"The Rabbit and the Lion"

by Ed Vuong

One night, Lion catches Rabbit. Lion wants to eat Rabbit, but Rabbit tricks Lion. He tells Lion to look in the well. Lion sees another lion in the well. It is lion's reflection. Lion shouts, "I am the king of the forest." He hears his echo: "I am the king of the forest." Lion is angry. He jumps into the well. Now Rabbit is safe.

WB
49–50

Key Words

In *The Contest,* North Wind and Sun find out who is stronger.

Words in Context 🎧

① Some **clouds** are puffy and light. Some clouds are dark and heavy. Which ones do you think bring rain?

② Which bridge is **stronger**?

What You Will Learn

Reading
- Vocabulary building: *Context, word study*
- Reading strategy: *Visualize*
- Text type: *Literature (fable)*

Grammar
Simple past: regular verbs

Writing
Retell a familiar story

These words will help you understand the reading.

Key Words

clouds

stronger

spiders

webs

brighter

3 Different kinds of <mark>spiders</mark> make different kinds of <mark>webs</mark>.

4 Which room is <mark>brighter</mark>?

Practice

Make flashcards to help you memorize the words.

- Write a key word on the front.
- On the back, write the meaning.

Make Connections

In this story, one character wants to win. Do you think winning is important? Why or why not? Discuss.

51

These words will help you talk about the reading.

Academic Words

affect
produce a change

attitude
way of thinking

Academic Words

Words in Context

The weather did not **affect** our trip. We were going no matter what.

Even though this class is difficult, we like it. We have a positive **attitude** about this class.

Practice

Choose an academic word to complete each sentence. Write your answer on the line.

1. Even when he loses, he doesn't get angry. He has a positive _____ about sports.

2. Don't look directly at the sun. It will _____ your eyes badly.

Apply

Ask and answer with a partner.

1. How does rain **affect** the way you feel?

2. How can a good **attitude** help you?

Word Study

Prefixes and Suffixes

A **prefix** is a word part added to the beginning of a word.

A **suffix** is a word part added to the end of a word.

Rule

Look for this pattern in English: when you add a prefix or suffix to a word, it changes the word's meaning. For example:

The prefix *dis* means *not*. So *dis*agree means *not agree*.

The suffix *less* means *without*. So rest*less* means *without rest*.

Practice

Read the sentences with a partner. Take turns.

- Tell the meaning of each word with the prefix *dis*.
- Tell the meaning of each word with the suffix *less*.

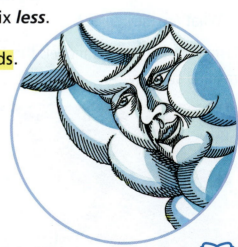

1. The sun is disappearing behind the clouds.

2. My sister and I disagree.

3. Mr. Ashton dislikes loud music.

4. At first the North Wind is thoughtless.

5. It's a beautiful, cloudless day.

WB
53

Literature
Fable

More About THE BiG QUESTION

Do you always need to be strong to meet a challenge?

🎧 **Listen to the Audio.**
Listen for the general meaning. Use the pictures to help you understand the selection.

Reading Strategy

Visualize

As you read, try to make pictures in your head.

- Where are the characters?
- What do they look like?
- What are they doing?

Listen as your teacher models the reading strategy.

The Contest

by Matt Aun
illustrated by Stephen Alcorn

The North Wind was **restless**. She wanted something to do.

"Look at the Sun," she thought. "All he does is shine. I can blow and move clouds to hide the Sun's light. I am stronger."

"Sun, who is stronger, you or I?" yelled the North Wind. She was always a little too loud. The Sun did not want to **argue**.

"We will have a contest," the North Wind howled.

"What kind?" asked the Sun.

---

restless not able to keep still

argue fight using words

Before You Go On

Close your eyes. Describe what the Sun and the North Wind look like.

The North Wind saw a woman walking on Earth. She wore a hat.

"Make that woman take off her hat," ordered the North Wind.

"You go first," said the Sun. The North Wind laughed. She thought the contest would be easy. She took a deep breath and blew. She pushed clouds to cover the Sun. She blew so hard the trees were bending. The ==spiders== held tight to their ==webs==.

But the woman walked on. She held on to her hat.

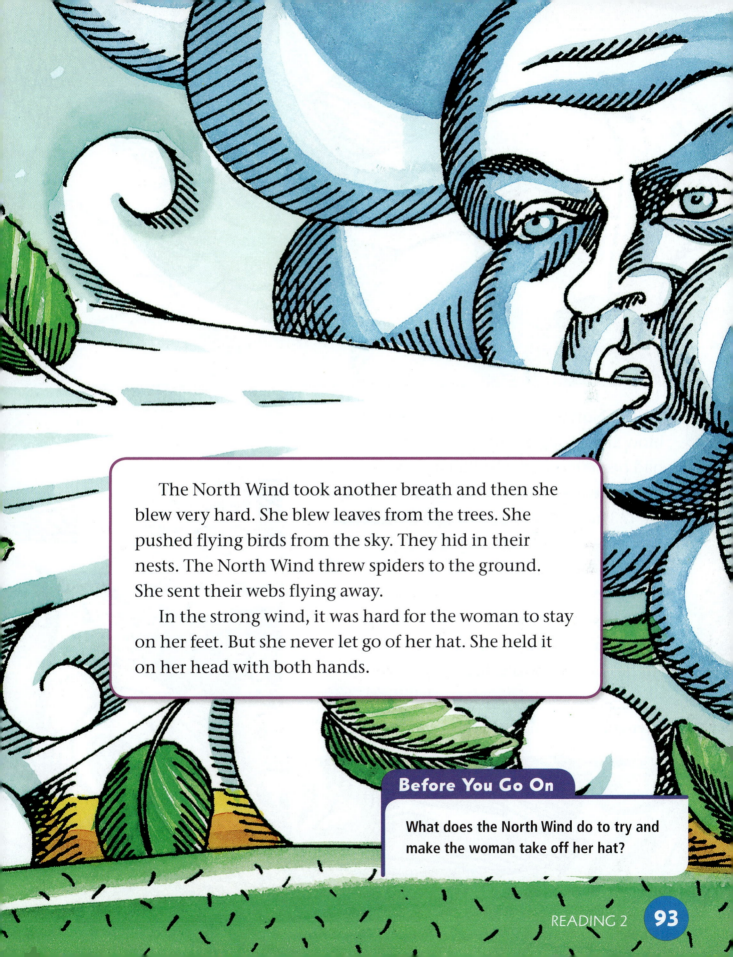

The North Wind took another breath and then she blew very hard. She blew leaves from the trees. She pushed flying birds from the sky. They hid in their nests. The North Wind threw spiders to the ground. She sent their webs flying away.

In the strong wind, it was hard for the woman to stay on her feet. But she never let go of her hat. She held it on her head with both hands.

Before You Go On

What does the North Wind do to try and make the woman take off her hat?

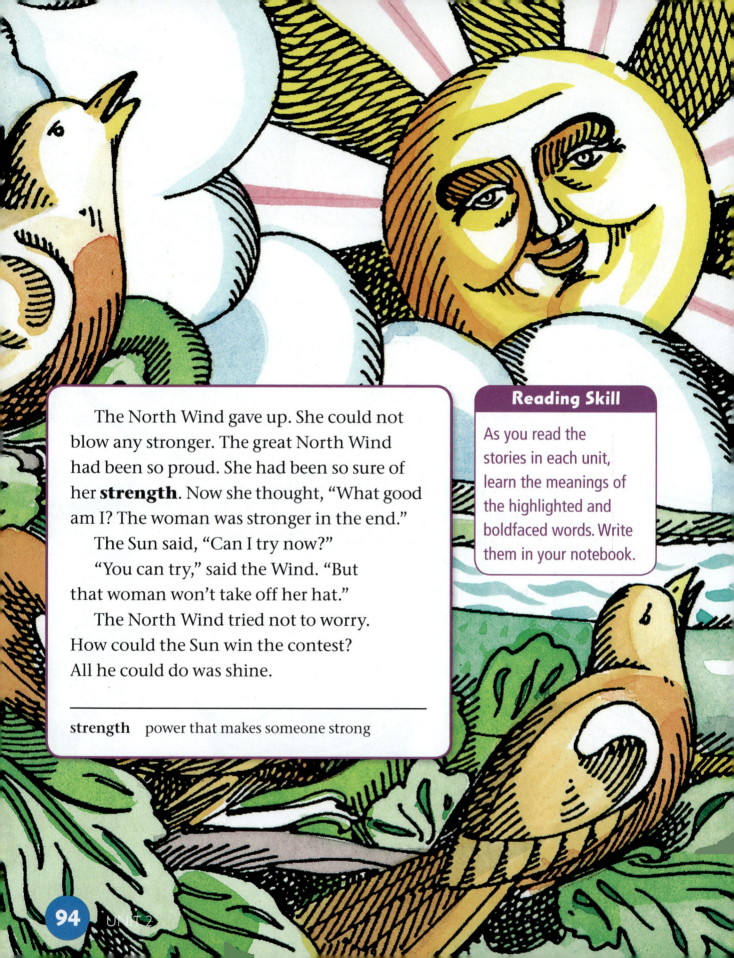

The North Wind gave up. She could not blow any stronger. The great North Wind had been so proud. She had been so sure of her **strength**. Now she thought, "What good am I? The woman was stronger in the end."

The Sun said, "Can I try now?"

"You can try," said the Wind. "But that woman won't take off her hat."

The North Wind tried not to worry. How could the Sun win the contest? All he could do was shine.

---

strength   power that makes someone strong

Reading Skill

As you read the stories in each unit, learn the meanings of the highlighted and boldfaced words. Write them in your notebook.

The Sun turned his face to Earth. He grew ==brighter==. The clouds disappeared. The Sun became even brighter. The birds peeked out of their nests. They started to sing. The spiders crawled back up the trees. They started to make new webs.

The woman stopped walking. She looked up.

Before You Go On

How does Sun **affect** the animals?

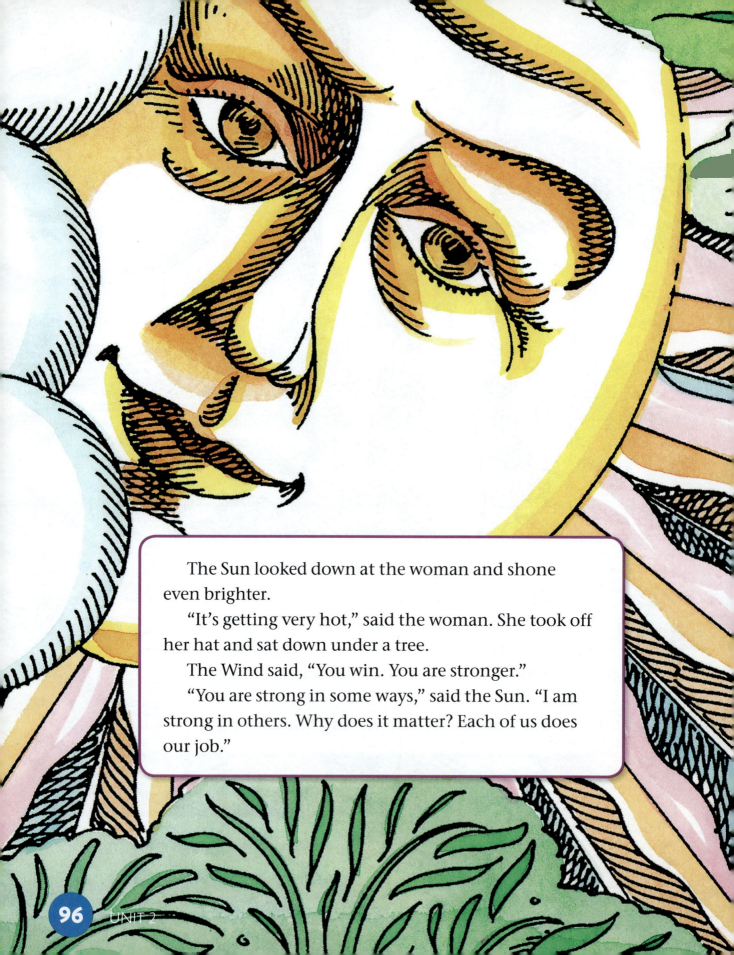

The Sun looked down at the woman and shone even brighter.

"It's getting very hot," said the woman. She took off her hat and sat down under a tree.

The Wind said, "You win. You are stronger."

"You are strong in some ways," said the Sun. "I am strong in others. Why does it matter? Each of us does our job."

The North Wind looked at the woman. The North Wind blew a tiny puff of air.

The woman smiled. She thought, "It's nice to have a cool **breeze** on such a hot day."

The North Wind smiled and thought, "Each of us does do our job."

---

breeze   light wind

Reading Strategy

Visualize

• Where are the Sun and North Wind?

• What do the Sun and North Wind look like?

• How did visualizing help you understand the story?

Think It Over

1. **Recall** What is the contest?

2. **Comprehend** Before the contest, what is North Wind's **attitude**?

3. **Analyze** After the contest, how does North Wind show that she has a new attitude?

WB 54–56

Learning Strategies

Visualizing

As you read, you can **visualize**, or make pictures in your head. You may make pictures of where the characters are. You may make pictures of what the characters look like. You may picture what is happening in the story.

Practice

Read each sentence. Describe the pictures you make in your mind. Choose one sentence and draw it.

1. The North Wind was restless. She wanted something to do.
2. The Sun turned his face to Earth. He grew brighter.
3. In the strong wind, it was hard for the woman to stay on her feet.

Draw the picture here.

Use a Compare and Contrast Chart

When you **compare,** you look for things that are the same. When you **contrast,** you look for things that are different. You can compare and contrast the different types of writing, or **genres** in this unit.

Practice
GO 12

List each of the statements below in the correct column of the chart. Some of the genres may have more than one statement.

Story	Play	Poem

57

- has events in a plot
- uses rhyme
- lists the name of the characters
- tells about conflicts

Apply

Retell the fable to a partner. Refer to the pictures as you speak.

Extension

Work in a group of four to act out *The Contest* as a play. One person is the director. The actors should follow the director's instructions. Present your play to the class.

Grammar

Simple Past: Regular Verbs

Use the simple past to talk about a completed action that happened before now.

> I **walked** away.   The woman **walked** away.
> She **talked** to Kim last night.   We **talked** to Kim last night.

Make the simple past of regular verbs by adding **-ed**.

> Add **-d** to verbs ending in -e.
>
> live ➝ **lived**

> Change the **y** to **i** and add **-ed** to verbs ending in a consonant and -y.
>
> try ➝ **tried**

> Add **-ed** to verbs ending in a vowel and -y.
>
> stay ➝ **stayed**

> **Double** the consonant and add **-ed** for verbs with a stressed CVC (consonant-vowel-consonant) ending.
>
> occur ➝ **occurred**

To make **negative sentences** in the past tense, use *did* + *not* + the base form of the verb.

> **Positive**   **Negative**
> We **laughed**. ➝ We **did not laugh**.
>
> did not ➝ **didn't**

To ask *Yes/No* **questions** in the past tense, begin the question with *did* + the subject + the base form of a verb.

> **Did** you stay?   Yes, I **did**.   Yes, I **stayed**.

Practice A

Use the past tense form of the verb in parentheses. Write the sentences.

1. He _____asked_____ a question. (ask)

2. The North Wind _____ the clouds around. (push)

3. The Sun _____ shining. (stop)

4. The heat _____ everyone. (affect)

5. The spiders _____ back to their webs. (crawl)

6. The girl _____ when she looked at the bright Sun. (cry)

Practice B

Change the sentences in Practice A into negative statements. Write the negative sentences in your notebook.

1. <u>He did not ask a question.</u>

Apply

Work with a partner. Ask and answer the questions about this week. Use simple past regular verbs in your answers.

Example: A: Did you call your friends this week?

B: Yes, I called them this week.

- Did your sister call a friend this week?
- Did a friend visit you at home?
- Did your brother watch television?
- Did you help your family?
- Did your friends study every day?

> **Grammar Check** ✔
>
> Name the **past tense** of three regular verbs.

58

Writing

Retell a Familiar Story

One way to write a narrative essay is to retell a familiar story in your own words.

Writing Prompt

Write a paragraph retelling a story you like. Use your own words. Describe what the characters say and do. Be sure to use the simple past correctly.

① Prewrite

Choose a story to retell. Who are the characters? What are the events that happen? List your ideas in a T-Chart.

A student named Reem listed her ideas like this:

HARE AND THE TORTOISE	
Beginnng	Hare and Tortoise agreed to race.
Middle	Hare raced quickly at first, then stopped and rested. Tortoise walked slowly and steadily.
End	Hare hurried to the finish line. Tortoise was already there.

② Draft

Use your T-Chart to help you write a draft.

• Keep in mind your purpose—to retell a familiar story.

• Include the beginning, the middle, and the end of the story.

③ Revise

Read your draft. Look for places where the writing needs improvement. Use the Writing Checklist to help you find problems. Then revise your draft.

④ Edit

Check your work for errors. Use the Peer Review Checklist on page 402.

⑤ Publish

Make a clean copy of your final draft. Share it with the class. Save your work. You will need it for the Writing Workshop.

Here is Reem's retelling of the story:

Writing Checklist

✔ **Ideas**
I included the events in the correct order.

I used my own words.

✔ **Conventions**
I used verbs in the past tense correctly.

I used punctuation and quotation marks correctly.

Reem Issa

Hare and Tortoise

Hare laughed at slow Tortoise.

"I can beat you in a race," he said. Tortoise answered, "Let's race and see." They started the race. Hare hopped away. He chased butterflies. Then he stopped under a tree and rested. Tortoise just walked and walked. Later, Hare opened his eyes. "Oh, no. I have to hurry." When Hare arrived at the finish line, Tortoise was already there.

W B
59–60

Key Words

Fresh Food in Strange Places is about how people are finding strange places to grow food.

Words in Context

There are different types of ==gardens== all over the world. People ==grow== fresh flowers and vegetables in the gardens.

First, they put seeds in the rich, dark soil, or ground. Then seeds grow into ==plants==. They water the plants. The plants grow and grow.

What You Will Learn

Reading
- Vocabulary building: *Context, phonics*
- Reading strategy: *Identify fact and opinion*
- Text type: *Informational text* (*social studies*)

Grammar
Simple past: *be* verbs

Writing
Write a journal entry about your day

These words will help you understand the reading.

Key Words

farm

fresh

grow

plants

garden

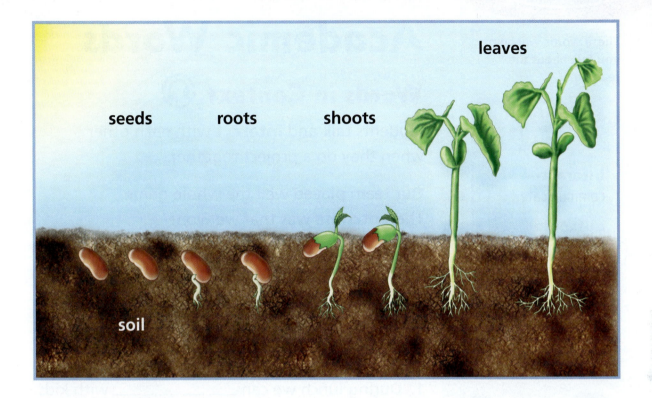

seeds　　roots　　shoots　　leaves

soil

Practice

Draw a picture of a neighborhood garden in your notebook. Label the picture using sentences that contain the key words.

Make Connections

Have you ever planted a seed for a flower or plant? How well did it grow? Would you like to work in a garden? After you discuss these questions, write your responses in your notebook.

61

These words will help you talk about the reading.

Academic Words

interact
communicate

outcome
result

Academic Words

Words in Context

Students talk and **interact** with each other when they do a project together.

Our team played well the whole game. The **outcome** was that we won!

Practice

Choose an academic word to complete each sentence.

1. During lunch we can _____ with kids from other grades.

2. When I study hard, the _____ is usually good.

Apply

Ask and answer with a partner.

1. What are some ways a child or an adult can **interact** with a baby?

2. What was the **outcome** of the last game you played?

Phonics

More Long Vowel Pairs

Long vowel pairs can make the long *a*, long *e*, or long *i* sounds. Listen. Then read each word aloud.

Long *a* Pairs		Long *e* Pairs		Long *i* Pair
day	rain	keep	neat	pie

Rule

When two vowels are together, the first vowel says its name.
- The letters *ai* or *ay* usually have the long *a* sound.
- The letters *ee* or *ea* usually have the long *e* sound.
- The letters *ie* usually have the long *i* sound.

Practice

Work with a partner. Take turns. Listen for words that have long vowel sounds.

Long *a*	Long *e*	Long *i*

Read the sentences below. Find and list in the chart the words with long vowel pairs.

1. Is that a bird in the tree?

2. What a long tail it has!

3. Pass the treat this way.

4. Let's have some pie.

Informational Text
Social Studies

🎧 **Listen to the Audio.**
Listen for the general meaning. Use the pictures to help you understand the selection.

Reading Strategy

Identify Fact and Opinion

A fact is something that is real or true. An opinion is what someone thinks.

- Identify statements in this reading that are facts. If it is a fact, you can prove it is true.

- Identify statements in this reading that are opinions. If it is an opinion, you cannot prove it is true or false.

Listen as your teacher models the reading strategy.

Fresh Food in Strange Places

There are now more than **7 billion** people in the world, and that number is getting a lot bigger. The **United Nations** says that the world's **population** will be 10 billion in the year 2055. With so many people in the world, how can we get enough food?

7 billion	7,000,000,000
population	number of people
United Nations	a group of almost 200 countries that work together

There are now more than 7 billion people in the world.

The population is not the only problem. In 1950, there were many more ==farms== around the world. Farms grow the food that we eat. Now, as cities get bigger and bigger, there are fewer farms. With fewer farms, it is harder for people in big cities to get ==fresh== food at good prices. Is it **possible** to ==grow== food in big cities? Many people think so.

---

possible   can be done

As cities get bigger, farms get smaller.

Before You Go On

What are some reasons it is harder for people to get fresh food?

At the Pasona Farm in Tokyo, Japan, food grows outside the building.

You can now find **urban** farms all over the world. Urban farms are places where people grow food together, but these "farms" are in big cities. Sometimes they are on a tall building or in a city park. The Pasona Farm in Tokyo, Japan, grows food inside an office building. They grow more than 200 kinds of vegetables, fruits, and rice. Some of the plants grow on the outside of the building. It looks strange, but it's a great idea!

---

urban   in a big city

A large building in The Hague, Netherlands, was full of **empty** offices. Now the building is the home of the Urban Farm de Schilde. This farm grows food on top of the building, and there is a fish farm at the bottom of the building. The Urban Farm de Schilde is an amazing place. They grow 45 **tons** of vegetables and raise 19 tons of fish every year. They sell their fresh **produce** and fish to supermarkets and restaurants in their city.

---

empty   has nothing inside

ton   1,000 kilograms

produce   fruits and vegetables

A man checks vegetable plants at the Urban Farm de Schilde in the Netherlands.

Before You Go On

What is the outcome of the farm in Netherlands?

Many schools around the world also have their own gardens and grow their own food. In school gardens, students learn about science while they grow vegetables and fruits. They also learn how to work together. The school then uses the produce to feed students in the school. Many students like trying the food that they grow!

Starting a farm or a garden is hard work, but it can also help many people. It can be fun, too! Does your school have a garden?

Students pick strawberries at a school garden in Denver, Colorado, U.S.A.

Dear Principal,

We would like to start a garden at our school. We want to grow all kinds of fruits and vegetables. We can eat some of the fresh food we grow, and we can also share it with people who do not have enough to eat.

In our garden, we will grow more than just plants. We will also grow friendships. Our garden will make our school stronger and more beautiful. It will make us healthier, too. We will have more fresh foods to eat, and we will get exercise as we work in our garden.

We would like to talk with you about our idea. We hope you like it!

Your students

W B 64–66

Think It Over

1. **Recall** What are people doing around the world to grow fresh food?

2. **Comprehend** What are some ways people can help others in their community?

3. **Analyze** How can growing fresh food make people **interact**?

Reading Strategy

Fact and Opinion

- Find two statements in the reading that are facts.

- Find two statements that are opinions.

Learning Strategies

Identify Fact and Opinion

A **fact** is something that can be proved. An **opinion** is what someone thinks.

- Statements of facts are points that are true. They can be proven.
- Statements of opinion are points that someone makes based on what they believe.

Practice

Tell whether the statements below are fact or opinion. Look carefully for clue words that help you decide. Remember that often an opinion is how someone feels, but can not be proven.

1. Fresh food is grown in a garden.
2. Plants can grow in many different types of places.
3. Everyone should have access to fresh food.
4. The garden must get sunlight. The sunlight helps the plants to grow.
5. Gardens must be watered on days it doesn't rain.

Use an Idea Web

An Idea Web can help you see how different ideas in a story are connected.

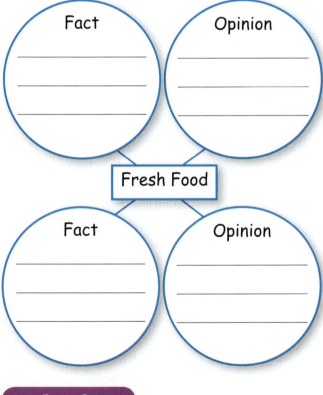

Practice GO 13

Reread *Fresh Food in Strange Places*. Copy the Idea Web in your notebook. Write down facts and opinions about strange places to grow food that you learned.

- Share your work with a partner.
- Discuss reasons why finding places to grow fresh food is a good idea.

Fact
_____
_____
_____

Opinion
_____
_____
_____

Fresh Food

Fact
_____
_____
_____

Opinion
_____
_____
_____

67

Extension

Think of a project you could start in your community, such as a community library, or a community recycling center. Write a letter inviting your neighbors to join your project. Display your letter in the classroom.

Apply

Summarize the selection. Use some of the key words as you speak.

Grammar

Simple Past: *Be* Verbs

Use the **simple past** of *be* to talk about events that started and finished in the past.

> The soil **is** ready. ⟶ The soil **was** ready yesterday.
> They **are** neighbors. ⟶ They **were** neighbors last year.

Simple past *be* verbs must agree with the subject.

Subject	Past
I	was
He/She/It	was
You/They/We	were

You can use **contractions** of *be* verbs in negative sentences.

> Our garden **wasn't** big.
> The chores **weren't** easy.

> was not ⟶ **wasn't**
> were not ⟶ **weren't**

To ask questions, put the *be* verbs before the **subject**.

> **Was** the **work** hard?
> Yes, it was. / No, it wasn't.
> **Were** the seeds fresh?
> Yes, they were. / No, they weren't.

Practice A

Go back to *Fresh Food in Strange Places* and circle the past form of the *be* verb.

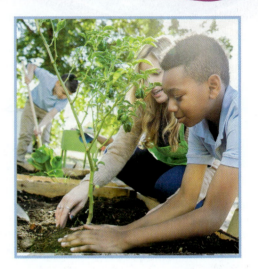

Practice B

Rewrite each sentence in your notebook using the simple past form of the *be* verb and the words in parentheses.

1. My classmates are at the park. (yesterday)

    My classmates were at the park yesterday.

2. I am tired. (last night)

    _____

3. Are you at the library? (two hours ago)

    _____

4. He is a gardener. (at his last job)

    _____

5. We are very busy today. (last week)

    _____

Apply

Work with a partner. Ask and answer questions about the school you went to last year. Use simple past *be* verbs in your answers.

68

Example: A: Who was your teacher?

B: My teacher was Ms. Garcia.

• Who were some of your friends?
• What was your favorite subject?

Grammar Check ✔

Write a question using a **simple past *be* verb**.

Writing

Write a Journal Entry about Your Day

A journal entry is another type of narrative essay.

> ### Writing Prompt
> Write a paragraph telling about something that happened to you. Say how you felt. Be sure to use the simple past of be correctly.

① **Prewrite** GO 12

Think about a day in the past. What did you do? Who did you see? List everything in a Three-Column Chart.

A student named Emily listed her ideas like this:

FACTS	SENSORY DETAILS	EMOTIONS
My teacher put a test on my desk. →	My brain was frozen. →	I was nervous.
My teacher asked, "Are you OK?" →	I couldn't move. →	I was scared.
My teacher smiled. →	My body relaxed. →	I felt better.

② **Draft**

Use your Three-Column Chart to help you write a first draft.
- Keep in mind your purpose—to write a journal entry.
- Write about how you felt and what you remember.

③ Revise

Reread your draft. Look for places where it needs improvement. Use the Writing Checklist to help you find problems. Then revise your draft.

④ Edit

Check your work for errors. Use the Peer Review Checklist on page 402.

⑤ Publish

Make a clean copy of your final draft. Share it with the class. Save your work. You will need it for the Writing Workshop.

Writing Checklist

✓ **Ideas**
I included the events in the correct order.

I expressed my ideas clearly.

✓ **Voice**
I wrote about how I felt.

✓ **Conventions**
I used verbs in the simple past tense correctly.

I used punctuation and quotation marks correctly.

Here is Emily's journal entry:

Wednesday, January 15th

I wasn't in school yesterday. This morning, my teacher put a math test on my desk. Suddenly I was nervous. I couldn't think. My brain was frozen. My teacher asked, "Are you OK?" But I couldn't move. I was scared. Then my teacher smiled. She said, "You weren't here yesterday. Don't worry. I'll help you." After that, my whole body relaxed. I felt much better.

69–70

Apply and Extend

Link the Readings

Read the words in the top row.

- For *The Rabbit and the Lion*, put an X under the words that remind you of the text.

- Repeat the same activity for the other readings.

	Informational text	Literature	Working together	Competition
The Rabbit and the Lion				
The Contest				
Fresh Food in Strange Places				

Discussion

1. In *The Rabbit and the Lion*, what is surprising about the **outcome** of the story?

2. Compare and contrast Rabbit with the Sun. How do their **attitudes** help them meet their challenges?

3. What are the rewards of working in a community garden?

All of us have challenges at times. How can people meet challenges?

> **Listening Skills**
>
> Take notes as you listen. Use your notes to ask questions.

Projects

Your teacher will help you choose one of these projects.

Written	Oral	Visual/Active
Email Write an email to a friend or relative. Tell that person about a problem you faced and how how you solved the problem.	**Talk and Help** Give an informal talk to children in first grade. Tell them about challenges you had when you were little and how you met them.	**What If Book** Create a picture book. Show ways to solve problems. For example, show a boy raising his hand to ask a question.
T-Chart Create a T-Chart for the selections in this unit. Use **Problem** and **Solution** as the headings.	**Act It Out** Work with a partner. Think of a problem to solve. Act out a scene about the problem, and then show the solution.	**Matching Game** Write a problem on five cards. Write a solution on five other cards. Have a partner try to match them.

71–72

Listening and Speaking Workshop
Perform a Skit

You are going to write and perform a skit. Then you will
listen as your classmates perform a skit, too.

① Prepare

A. Find two partners. Choose a scene
from one of the readings. Then act it
out as a skit.

B. Study your scene and decide where it
begins and ends. Who is going to play
each part? Now write your skit. Discuss
and find props to use in your skit.
As you work together, listen to each
other's ideas and work cooperatively.

Useful Language
Listen and Repeat.
We want to show you our skit.
Can you watch our skit, please?
Our skit is about . . . .
Ready?
So . . . . what do you think?
Did you like it?
Thank you!

	The Contest
North Wind:	Sun, who is stronger, you or I? We will have a contest.
Sun:	What kind?
North Wind:	Make that woman take off her hat.
Sun:	You go first.
Woman:	Oh, it's windy!

② Practice

Practice your skit with your props. Act it out in front of your family or friends. If possible, record your skit. Then listen to it. How do you and your partners sound? Record it again and try to improve.

③ Present

As you speak, do the following:

- Don't be nervous. Have fun.
- Don't read your skit—act it out.
- Pay attention to your partners, so you know when to say your lines.

As you listen, do the following:

- Watch the actions of the actors.
- Pay close attention. Your teacher will ask you questions after the skit.

④ Evaluate

After you speak, answer these questions:

✔ Did you act out your skit?

✔ Did you use props?

After you listen, answer these questions:

✔ Did you watch the actions of the actors?

✔ How did the actions help you understand?

✔ Was the skit formal or informal?

Speaking Skills

Skits can be about formal or informal situations. Use formal or informal language based on the story.

Listening Skills

Listen carefully for the situation and events of the skit. This will help you understand it better.

Writing Workshop
Write a Story

Writing Prompt

Write a story. Include everything that happened and how you felt. List the main details in a graphic organizer.

① Prewrite

Review the writing you have done in this unit. Now choose something that happened to you to write about. Include vivid details. List what happened in a graphic organizer.

A student named Gabriel listed his ideas like this:

> **Beginning:**
> I heard a funny noise coming from the attic.

↓

> **Middle:**
> I decided to investigate. I went up the attic stairs.

↓

> **End:**
> It was a mouse caught in a trap.

② Draft

Use your chart to help you write a first draft.

• Keep in mind your purpose—to tell a story.

• Include what happened and how you felt.

③ Revise

Read your draft. Look for places where the writing needs improvement. Use the Writing Checklist to help you find problems. Then revise your draft.

Here is how Gabriel revised his essay:

Six Traits of Writing Checklist

 Ideas
Does my story include vivid details?

 Organization
Does my story have a beginning, middle, and end?

 Voice
Does my language express my feelings?

 Word Choice
Did I use specific words?

 Sentence Fluency
Did I use different kinds of sentences?

 Conventions
Do pronouns agree with their subjects?

Gabriel Velazquez

The Noise in the Attic

One morning last winter I was lying in bed. It was still dark. I was almost asleep.

Suddenly, I heard something over my head. It was coming from the attic. It sounded like something being ~~draged~~ dragged across the floor. I decided to investigate.

> **Revised** to correct spelling error.

I took my plastic pirate sword for protection. I slowly ~~walk~~ walked up the stairs. I was cold and afraid. Everything was quiet, but I could still hear the dragging noise. Slowly, I opened the door and looked around ~~the door.~~ to see what was there.

> **Revised** to create verb tense.

> **Revised** to make the meaning clearer.

It was a mouse caught by his tail! I let him go outside. I felt very brave!

④ Edit

Check your work for errors. Trade papers with a partner to get feedback. Use the Peer Review Checklist.

⑤ Publish

Make a clean copy of your final draft. Share it with the class.

73–74

Peer Review Checklist

✔ The events are clear and in an order that makes sense.

✔ The writing is interesting and engaging.

✔ The subjects and verbs agree.

Spelling Tip

In a one-syllable word, if the word ends in a CVC pattern, double the consonant before you add *-ed (drag ⟶ dragged)*.

Fluency

Listen to the sentences. Pay attention to the groups of words. Read aloud.

1. A small, smart rabbit can trick a big, strong lion.

2. Everyone can use their strengths to do a good job.

3. If we work together, we can create a beautiful garden.

Work in pairs. Take turns reading aloud the passage below for one minute. Count the number of words you read.

The Contest tells about a competition between the North Wind	10
and the Sun. They see a woman wearing a hat. The North Wind	23
says she will make the lady take off her hat. She blows very hard	37
but the woman holds on to her hat. Then the Sun tries. The Sun	51
grows hotter and brighter. The woman is hot, so she takes off	63
her hat. The North Wind says the Sun is stronger. The Sun says	76
they do their job.	80

With your partner, find the words that slowed you down.

- Practice saying each word and then say the sentence each word is in.

- Then take turns reading the text again. Count the number of words you read.

Taking Tests

You will often take tests that help show what you know. Follow these tips to improve your test-taking skills.

> ### Coaching Corner
>
> **Answering Test Questions**
>
> - When answering a multiple-choice question, watch out for answer choices that are similar to the correct answer. Think hard about what the question is asking and choose the *best* answer.
>
> - Before you read a selection, preview the questions that go with the selection. Reading the questions first will help you think about the information you need while you read the selection. After you finish reading the selection, read the questions again to help you choose the best answer.
>
> - Before you answer a question based on a picture, read the question carefully. Be sure you understand what the question is asking. Study every part of the picture closely before you choose an answer.

W B
77–78

Read the selection. Study the tips in the Coaching Corner. Then answer the questions.

Prickly Pears

The desert can be a challenging place to live. But the prickly pear cactus is a tough plant! Although the desert only gets a few inches of rain each year, prickly pears can grow to be up to 10 feet tall. Prickly pears have special leaves that store water to keep them healthy in very hot and dry weather. These plants are also covered with sharp, yellow spines to protect them from predators.

1 Which part of a prickly pear cactus helps protect it from animals?

A leaves

B pears

C water

D spines

2 Which of the following sentences is an opinion?

F The prickly pear cactus is a tough plant!

G Prickly pears can grow to be 10 feet tall.

H Prickly pears have special leaves that store water.

J These plants are covered with sharp, yellow spines.

Tips
✔ Be careful. All of the answer choices are words from the selection. Only one is correct.
✔ Remember that a fact is always true. An opinion is what someone thinks, but it may not be true.

Animals in Nature

What animals change shape as they grow? What do alligators eat? What animals hide right in their surroundings? Read on to find out!

Reading 1
Poem

Animal Habitats

Reading 2
Photo Essay

Can You See Them?

Reading 3
Science

How Do They Grow?

THE BiG QUESTION

What can we learn about animals and why is learning about them important?

Listening and Speaking

You will talk about animals and how they live. In the Listening and Speaking Workshop, you will recite a poem.

Writing

You will practice narrative writing. In the Writing Workshop, you will write a personal narrative.

Quick Write

What is your favorite animal? Write some things you like about this animal.

View and Respond

Talk about the poster for this unit. Then watch and listen to the video and answer the questions at Pearson English Portal.

Words to Know

Listen and repeat. Use these words to talk about animals.

frog

monkey

raccoon

squirrel

butterfly

horse

Practice

Work with a partner. Look up these words in a dictionary. Then ask and answer questions.

climb	fly	jump	run

Example: A: What can <u>squirrels</u> do?

B: They can <u>climb</u>.

Write

Read the question. Write your response in your notebook.

What animals do you usually see in parks? On farms? In zoos?

Make Connections

Complete the sentences.

woods

pond

rain forest

1. A: This animal lives near a _____ and likes to jump in the water.

  B: It's a frog.

2. A: This animal lives in the _____. It climbs trees and eats nuts.

  B: It's a squirrel.

3. A: This animal lives in the _____ and likes to jump from tree to tree.

  B: It's a monkey.

What about you?

Talk with a partner. Choose an animal. Tell your partner where it lives and what it does. Then guess each other's animal.

Build Unit Background

Kids' Stories from around the World 🎧

U.S.A.

Senegal

Cassie

I live near the Everglades National Park in Florida, U.S.A. There are lots of insects in the park. That's good, because I like insects. This yellow grasshopper is called an eastern lubber. I see a lot of these grasshoppers in the summer.

Obiajulu

I live near the Niokolo-Koba National Park in Senegal. I can hear the running frog at a pond near my home. Its voice sounds like water dropping in a pail. The running frog does not hop like other frogs. It runs!

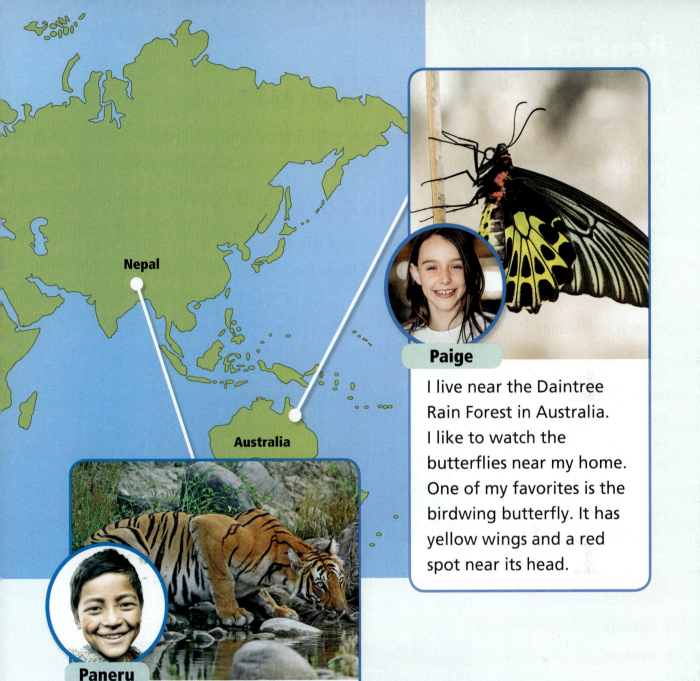

Paige

I live near the Daintree Rain Forest in Australia. I like to watch the butterflies near my home. One of my favorites is the birdwing butterfly. It has yellow wings and a red spot near its head.

Paneru

I live near the Chitwan National Park in Nepal. Tigers live in this park. There are not many tigers left in Nepal. People have hunted them. Today, forest rangers are working hard to protect the tigers.

What about you?

1. What animals do you see where you live?

2. Do you have a story about an animal where you live? Share your story.

What You Will Learn

Reading
- Vocabulary building: *Context, phonics*
- Reading strategy: *Make inferences*
- Text type: *Literature (poem)*

Grammar
Prepositions and prepositional phrases

Writing
Write a poem

These words will help you understand the reading.

Key Words

camels

amazing

habits

caves

plains

Key Words

Animal Habitats tells about animals and where they live.

Words in Context

1 <mark>Camels</mark> live in the desert. Some camels have two humps on their backs. Other camels have just one hump.

2 The flying squirrel is <mark>amazing</mark>. It does not fly. It jumps and glides through the air.

3 Eating fruit and vegetables and washing your hands before eating are good health <mark>habits</mark> to follow.

4 Some bears live in <mark>caves</mark>. This bear looks out from a cave on the side of a mountain.

5 Bison live on the wide, flat <mark>plains</mark> of North America.

Practice

Add a page to your vocabulary notebook.
- Divide your page into three columns: the new words, their definitions, and drawings of the words (whenever possible).
- Test yourself by covering one of the columns.

Make Connections

Some animals live in <mark>caves</mark>. Some live on <mark>plains</mark>. What animals live near you? Where do they live?

79

These words will help you talk about the reading.

Academic Words

appreciate
like or understand the value of something

illustrate
show

Academic Words

Words in Context

My mom knows I **appreciate** her cooking because I always say "thank you" after dinner.

The stories **illustrate** interesting places where animals live.

Practice

Choose an academic word to complete each sentence.

1. How do you _____ how happy you are?

2. Learning how to play an instrument helps us to _____ music more.

Apply

Ask and answer with a partner.

1. How do you show your friends that you **appreciate** them?

2. What book **illustrates** the kind of story you like to read?

Phonics

Consonant Clusters

Sometimes when two consonants are together, each consonant keeps its own sound. Listen. Then read each word aloud.

r-blends	l-blends	s-blends
frog	fly	sky
trees	plains	swim

Rule

Blend the sounds of both letters when a word has
- a consonant followed by the letter *r*
- a consonant followed by the letter *l*
- the letter *s* followed by another consonant

Practice

Work with a partner.

- Choose a word from the chart above to answer each question. Write the answers in your notebook. Use complete sentences.
- Circle each *r*-blend, *s*-blend, or *l*-blend in your answers.

1. Where do monkeys live?

2. What lives in a pond?

3. What do sharks do?

4. What rhymes with *sky*?

81

Literature

Poem

More About THE BiG QUESTION

Why should people care where animals live?

🎧 **Listen to the Audio.**

Listen for the general meaning. Think about the situation or context. Use this to help you understand the poems.

Reading Strategy

Make Inferences

Making inferences helps you figure out information that the author doesn't say directly.

- As you read, think about the different animals.
- Think about why each animal lives where it does.

Listen as your teacher models the reading strategy.

Animal Habitats

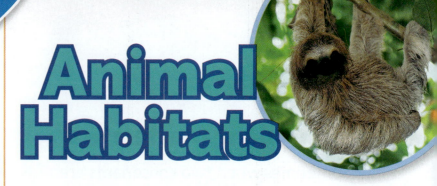

Animal **habitats** can be found all around us;
In caves and water, with flat plains and trees.
Animals live where their needs can be met.
They can roam wherever they please.

The rainforest is a hot and rainy place.
It is home to half of the world's creatures.
Sloths and snakes call this place home.
The rainforest has unusual **features**.
The desert is a place where it's hot and dry.
No animal, it seems, could ever survive here
for long. This habitat is full of creatures, big
and small — But snakes, camels, and foxes
all seem to belong!

---

habitat the environment where an animal usually lives

features important parts or characteristics of something

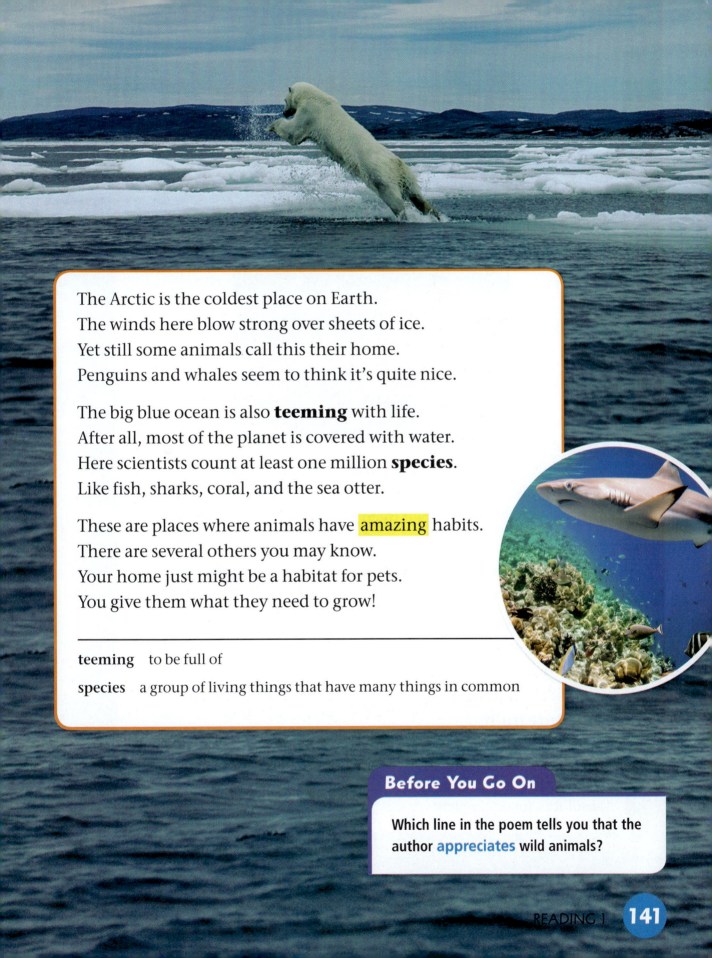

The Arctic is the coldest place on Earth.
The winds here blow strong over sheets of ice.
Yet still some animals call this their home.
Penguins and whales seem to think it's quite nice.

The big blue ocean is also **teeming** with life.
After all, most of the planet is covered with water.
Here scientists count at least one million **species**.
Like fish, sharks, coral, and the sea otter.

These are places where animals have amazing habits.
There are several others you may know.
Your home just might be a habitat for pets.
You give them what they need to grow!

---

teeming   to be full of

species   a group of living things that have many things in common

Before You Go On

Which line in the poem tells you that the author **appreciates** wild animals?

Alligators and Crocodiles

Alligators and crocodiles, they have similar features.

They are also not alike, they are different creatures.

Alligators have a U-shaped head, the crocodiles' are shaped like a V.

Alligators prefer **freshwater**, crocodiles swim in the sea.

Alligators have darker skin, the crocodile's skin is lighter.

Alligators are pretty nice, while the crocodile is a fighter.

Both animals have a mouth full of chompers, but crocodiles have one funny tooth;

That sticks out when its mouth is closed, and that is the **absolute** truth.

---

freshwater   water that is not from the ocean

absolute   total; complete

Tongue Twister:

Grumpy green gators **gobble grubs** in the grass.

Riddles:

What was the alligator doing on the highway?

   About two miles an hour.

---

gobble   eat

grubs   larva that look like thick worms

How many alligators does it take to drive a car?

   Three. One to steer. One to push the pedals. And one to yell out the window, "Get out of the way! Don't you know alligators can't drive?"

82–84

Think It Over

1. **Recall** What are the two ways animals share the world with us?

2. **Comprehend** What lines in the poem **illustrate** how alligators and crocodiles are similar?

3. **Analyze** How is the description of animal homes different in the two poems?

Reading Strategy
Make Inferences

- Why do you think different kinds of animals have different kinds of homes?

- What can you infer about the crocodiles?

▲ Eggs in a nest
A mother alligator lays many eggs in a nest.

▲ Hatching
A baby alligator hatches. It comes out of its shell.

▲ Going to water
The mother alligator takes the baby alligator to water. Babies know how to swim right away by instinct.

▲ Free ride
This baby alligator rests on its mother's head.

▲ Friends

This young alligator shares a log with a painted turtle. But the turtle needs to be careful.

▲ Food

A grown alligator eats turtles. Alligators like to eat fish, too. An alligator uses its teeth to catch food. It does not chew the food. It swallows the food whole.

▲ Sunning themselves

Alligators are usually in or near water. Alligators warm themselves in the sun. This one rests on rocks in a swamp.

Activity to Do

These two pages use pictures and captions (words) to tell you about alligators.

- Choose another animal.
- Find pictures of the animal and write captions.
- Post your pictures and captions in your classroom.

Learning Strategies

Inferences

You make **inferences** when you figure out something as you read.

Practice

Make inferences about the poem *Animal Habitats.*

- Read the poem.
- Put together what you know and what you read.

> These are some places where <mark>amazing</mark> animals can live.
> There are several others you may know.
> Your home just might be a habitat for pets.
> You give them what they need to grow!

1. How do pets share the world with us?
2. How do wild animals share the world with us?
3. How is your home a habitat for pets?

Use a K-W-L Chart

You can use a K-W-L Chart to make inferences. K-W-L stands for What You **Know**, What You **Want** to Know, and What You **Learned**.

Practice GO 5

Answer the questions below.
Your answers will help you fill in the chart.
Write your answers in the chart.

What You Know	What You Want to Know	What You Learned
The poem says "Animal habitats can be found all around us."	How do animals and people share the world?	People need to appreciate wild animals and where they live.
The poem says that "amazing" animals live in different places.	_____ _____ _____ _____	_____ _____ _____ _____

1. What is special about animals' homes? Why are these animals "amazing"?
2. How does the poet feel about animals?

W B
85

Apply

Summarize the poem *Animal Habitats* for a partner. Include inferences you have made about the poem in your summary. Use some of the key words.

Extension

Work in pairs. Choose an animal. Do research independently on where the animal lives and what it eats. Share your information with your partner. Create a chart together. Share it with the class.

Grammar

Prepositions of Location

A **preposition of location** tells where something is.

> Crocodiles live **in** lakes.

A preposition is always followed by a **noun** or **pronoun**. A preposition +
a noun or pronoun is called a **prepositional phrase**. For example, **at home**
and **in the ocean** are both prepositional phrases.

The noun or pronoun that follows a preposition is called an **object of
the preposition**.

> Bats live **in caves**.

Review these common prepositions of location and prepositional phrases.

Preposition	Prepositional Phrases
in	**in** caves / **in** the water / **in** Australia
on	**on** a table / **on** the floor / **on** a leaf
at	**at** home / **at** school / **at** the park
between	**between** the tree and the river
near	**near** the zoo / **near** the plains
under	**under** the tree / **under** the desk
above	**above** the mountain / **above** the door
in front of	**in front of** the house / **in front of** the class
behind	**behind** the house / **behind** me
next to	**next to** that tree / **next to** him

Practice A

Complete the sentences with *on*, *at*, *between*, *under*, or *above*.

1. We have a rabbit __at__ school.

2. We see squirrels _____ the park.

3. Monkeys jump _____ the trees.

4. The camels walked _____ the sand.

5. The cat ran _____ the bed!

6. The horses are _____ the trees and the river.

Practice B

Underline the prepositional phrase in each sentence in Practice A.

Apply

Work with a partner. Ask and answer the questions. Use prepositional phrases in your answers.

Example: A: What do you have on your desk?

B: I have a notebook on my desk.

- Where do you eat lunch?
- Where do you like to play with friends?
- What do you keep in your backpack?
- Where do you live?
- Where do you keep your toys and games?
- Where do you sit in class?
- Where do you do your homework?

Grammar Check ✔

Name a **preposition**.
Use it in a sentence.

86

Writing

Write a Poem about an Animal

A poem can express ideas, information, and feelings. A good poem includes details that help the reader picture what is being described.

Writing Prompt

Write a poem about an animal. Tell facts about the animal. Be sure to use prepositions of location correctly.

① Prewrite

Choose an animal to write about. Think about the animal's habits. What does the animal eat? Where does it live and sleep? List the facts in a Poem Chart.

A student named Antonio has started to list his ideas like this:

LINE 1:	I am a/an (<u>animal</u>).	I am a bat.
LINE 2:	I am as (<u>color</u>) as (<u>noun</u>).	I am as black as the night.
LINE 3:	I live in (<u>place</u>).	I live in caves and in tree tops.
LINE 4:	I eat (<u>foods</u>).	I eat insects and fruit.

② Draft

Use your Poem Chart to help you write a first draft.
- Keep in mind your purpose—to write a poem.
- Include interesting facts about your animal.

③ Revise

Reread your draft. Look for places where it needs improvement. Use the Writing Checklist to help you find problems. Then revise your draft.

④ Edit

Check your work for errors. Do Peer Review (use the Checklist on page 402).

⑤ Publish

Make a clean copy of your final draft. Share it with the class. Save your work for the Writing Workshop.

Here is Antonio's poem:

Writing Checklist

✓ **Ideas**
I included facts in my poem.
I expressed my ideas clearly.

✓ **Word Choice**
I included descriptive words.

✓ **Conventions**
I used prepositions and prepositional phrases correctly.

Antonio Corrales

I am a bat.
I am as black as the night.
I live in caves and in tree tops.
I eat insects and fruit.
I sleep upside down during the day with
other bats.
I can fly through the air.
I can see in the dark.
I am a bat.

Key Words

Can You See Them? tells how animals use camouflage.

Words in Context

1 This is an <mark>insect</mark>. An insect has three body parts, six legs, and antennae. Insects may also have wings.

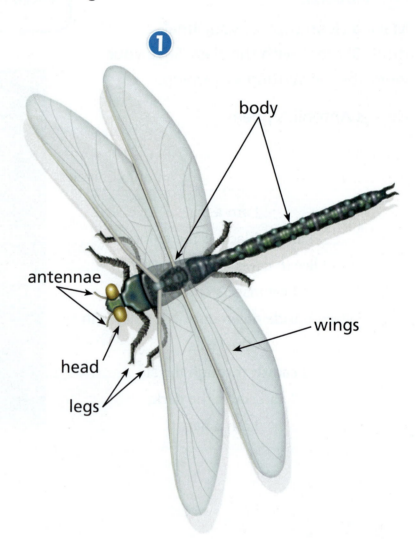

body

antennae

head

legs

wings

2 **Habitats** are where animals live. Animals use **camouflage** to hide in their habitats. They hide from other animals that might eat them. Also, animals hide so they can catch prey. **Prey** is any animal that another animal eats.

3 The **patterns** on the pepper **moth** help it hide on a tree.

Practice

Make flashcards to help you memorize the words.

- Write a key word on the front.
- On the back, write the meaning.

Make Connections

Some animals use **camouflage** to be safe. People wear seat belts in cars to be safe. What do you do to be safe?

Speaking Skills

When you don't know the right word to use, explain or describe the idea using words you know.

89

These words will help you talk about the reading.

Academic Words

Words in Context

Frogs need to live in a wet **environment**.

Wings **enable** birds to fly.

Practice

Choose an academic word to complete each sentence.

1. People should keep the _____ clean.

2. Reading books will _____ you to learn about animals.

Apply

Ask and answer with a partner.

1. What is a good **environment** for a pet?

2. What **enables** flowers to grow?

Word Study
Compound Nouns

A **compound noun** consists of two or more shorter words to form a new word.

butterfly	**rainforest**	**grasshopper**
butter + fly	rain + forest	grass + hopper

Rule

Look for this pattern in English: Sometimes two nouns join to form a new noun. These new nouns are called *compound nouns*.

Practice

Work with a partner. Take turns.

- Read the sentences.
- List the compound nouns.
- Show the two words that make up each compound noun.

1. Squirrels live in the woodlands.

2. Owls sleep during the daylight.

3. At nightfall, raccoons come out to look for food.

Informational Text
Photo Essay

Why is it important to know how animals use camouflage?

🎧 **Listen to the Audio.**
Listen for the general meaning. Think about the situation or context. Use this to help you understand the selection.

Reading Strategy

Identify Cause and Effect

Identifying cause and effect helps you understand how things are connected.

- As you read, look for causes—things that make other things happen.

- Look for effects—things that happen because of something else.

Listen as your teacher models the reading strategy.

Can You See Them?

by Kendra Clay

Can you see the insect in the photograph above? You will need to look carefully.

The insect is called a walking stick. It can hide in a tree because it looks like a small branch, or stick.

Arctic foxes live where the weather is very cold. They can change color. In summer, the foxes are brown. In winter, they are white.

Many animals hide. They may hide to keep safe from **predators**. Or, they may hide so they can catch prey.

This kind of hiding is called camouflage. When animals have camouflage, they are hard to see in their habitats.

---

pounces   jumps suddenly after waiting

predators   animals that kill and eat other animals

A tawny frogmouth is a bird. It sits very still in a tree. It waits for prey to come near. Then it **pounces**!

Patterns help this moth stay safe. Look at the big spots on the moth's wings. They look like a large animal's eyes. Predators stay away from this insect.

Before You Go On

Why does the tawny frogmouth stay very still?

A horned lizard is the color of the ground. The lizard can quickly change from a light color to a dark color. The insects it eats do not know it is there.

Sandhill cranes **migrate** south from Canada and Alaska. These gray-and-white birds blend in with the snowy lands around them.

A Bengal tiger is a very large cat. It's hard for a big animal to hide. But the tiger has stripes. In the tiger's habitat, its stripes blend in with the plants.

migrate   move from one area to another as the seasons change

A leaf-tailed gecko is a kind of lizard. It blends in with a tree branch in Africa. It waits for prey to fly by.

This cottontail rabbit hides in some leaves on the ground in the forest. It must hide from predators.

92–94

Reading Strategy

Identify Cause and Effect

- Did you find out why some animals use camouflage?
- How did looking for cause and effect help you understand the selection?

Think It Over

1. **Recall** In what kind of climate do arctic foxes live?

2. **Comprehend** What does camouflage enable animals to do?

3. **Analyze** What role does environment play in an animal's ability to hide?

Learning Strategies

Cause and Effect

In a cause-and-effect situation, the **cause** is the reason why something happens; and the **effect** is the result of what happened.

Practice

Draw a line from each effect to its cause.

Cause	Effect
1. The Bengal tiger has stripes.	a. It can hide in a tree.
2. The Arctic fox lives where there is snow.	b. It can hide in the tall grass.
3. The walking stick insect looks like a small branch.	c. It can hide in the winter when its coat turns white.

Use a Cause and Effect Chart

Use a Cause and Effect Chart to show how camouflage helps animals.

Practice
GO 7

Read the information in the chart.

- For each cause, write the effect.
- Add two more causes and their effects.

Cause	Effect
The Bengal tiger has stripes.	It can hide in the tall grass.
The Arctic fox lives where there is snow.	
The walking stick looks like a branch.	

95

Apply

Summarize the selection to a partner.

Extension

Invent an animal with special camouflage. Label the picture to show how the camouflage helps your animal to stay safe. Share your drawing with the class.

Grammar

Adjectives and Adverbs

An **adjective** describes a noun. Adjectives give details about size, shape, color, and number. They also express observations and opinions.

a **tall** giraffe (*size*)	**three** horses (*number*)
round eyes (*shape*)	**smooth** fur (*observation*)
a **white** fox (*color*)	a **funny** joke (*opinion*)

In sentences, adjectives can go **before** a noun or **after** the verb *be*.

Before a noun		After the verb *be*
The <mark>moth</mark> has **big** <u>spots</u>.	→	Those spots **are big**.
Look at the **brown** <u>insect</u>.	→	The insect **is brown**.
Do you like **cold** <u>weather</u>?	→	The weather **is cold**.

An **adverb** modifies a **verb**, an **adjective,** or another **adverb**. Many adverbs answer the question *How?* These adverbs often end in *–ly*.

Adverbs ending in *-ly*:	Other adverbs:
You need to look **carefully**.	The weather is **very** cold.
The lizard can **quickly** change.	The tiger is **quite** dangerous.
The gecko waits **quietly** for a meal.	

Practice A

Circle the adjectives in the sentences.

1. The (green) gecko is hiding.

2. The large tiger has black stripes.

3. The quiet moth is very still.

4. The brown rabbit quietly hid in the soft leaves.

5. The tiny lizard quickly changed color.

6. The hungry hawk swooped down on its prey.

Practice B

Underline the adverbs in the sentences in Practice A.

Apply

**Work with a partner. Ask and answer the questions.
Use adjectives and adverbs in your sentences.**

Example: A: What color is your hair?

B: My hair is brown.

- What kind of weather do you like?
- What does your friend's dog look like?
- Do you have a big collection of anything?
- Do you walk quickly or slowly?
- Do you talk loudly or softly?
- Do you exercise daily or weekly?
- Do you ride your bike carefully
  or carelessly?

> **Grammar Check** ✔
>
> Name one **adjective**
> and one **adverb**. Use
> each one in a sentence.

WB
96

Writing

Write a Friendly Letter

When you write a letter, you must think about your audience. Who will be reading your letter? This will affect your choice of words and language structures.

Writing Prompt

Write a letter to a friend or family member. Use informal language. Talk about something that you are learning in school. Be sure to use adjectives and adverbs correctly.

① Prewrite

Choose an animal or insect to write about. Think about its physical characteristics and/or habits. Then think about what these characteristics allow it to do. List the facts in a chart.

A student named Iman listed his ideas like this:

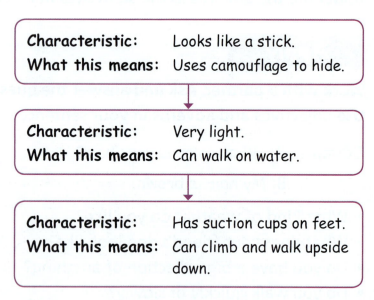

Characteristic: Looks like a stick.
What this means: Uses camouflage to hide.

Characteristic: Very light.
What this means: Can walk on water.

Characteristic: Has suction cups on feet.
What this means: Can climb and walk upside down.

② Draft

Use your chart to help you write a first draft.

- Keep in mind your purpose–to write a friendly letter.
- Include interesting facts about your animal or insect.

③ Revise

Reread your draft. Look for places where it needs improvement. Use the Writing Checklist to help you find problems. Then revise your draft.

④ Edit

Check your work for errors. Do Peer Review (use the Checklist on page 402).

⑤ Publish

Make a clean copy of your final draft. Share it with the class. Save your work for the Writing Workshop.

Here is Ahmed's letter:

Writing Checklist

✓ **Ideas**
I included facts in my letter.
I expressed my ideas clearly.

✓ **Conventions**
I used adjectives correctly.
I used adverbs correctly.

41 Oak Road

Bigtown, MD 09050

March 14, 2019

Dear Grandma,

    I learned about a really interesting insect in school today. Have you ever seen a walking stick? It's an insect that looks exactly like a tree branch or twig. It uses camouflage, so birds can't find it. A walking stick moves very slowly. Amazingly, it can walk on water! It has claws and suction cups on its feet, so it can walk upside down. Isn't that cool?

Love,

Ahmed

97–98

Reading 3
Prepare to Read

Key Words

How Do They Grow? tells how a butterfly and a frog change as they grow.

Words in Context

A **butterfly** changes as it grows.

1 It starts as an egg on a **leaf**.

2 The egg begins to **hatch**.

3 A **caterpillar**, or larva, comes out of the egg. It eats and eats.

4 The caterpillar becomes fully grown and hangs from a leaf or branch.

5 It makes a pupa, or chrysalis.

6 The chrysalis opens and a butterfly comes out.

What You Will Learn

Reading
- Vocabulary building: *Context, phonics*
- Reading strategy: *Identify sequence*
- Text type: *Informational text (science)*

Grammar
Adverbs of time

Writing
Write a personal narrative

These words will help you understand the reading.

Key Words

butterfly
leaf
hatch
caterpillar
tadpole

A frog also changes. A <mark>tadpole</mark> is a baby frog. It changes into a frog when it grows up.

Practice

Draw pictures of the key words. Label each picture with a sentence that contains the key word.

Make Connections

Some animals change as they grow. How do you change as you grow? How do you feel about these changes? After you discuss these questions, write your responses in your notebook.

99

These words will help you talk about the reading.

occurs
happens

transform
completely change

Academic Words

Words in Context

When the eggs break open, something special **occurs**. Baby chicks are born.

A small caterpillar **transforms** into a beautiful butterfly.

Practice

Choose an academic word to complete each sentence.

1. Water _____ into ice when you put it in the freezer.

2. What major international sports event _____ every four years?

Apply

Ask and answer with a partner.

1. What are some things that **occur** at your school every day?

2. If you could **transform** yourself into an animal, which animal would you be? Explain.

100

Phonics

Digraphs: *ch, sh, th*

Sometimes when two consonants are together, they make a new sound. Listen. Then read each word aloud.

ch	sh	th
change	ship	then
branch	wish	both

Rule

The letters *ch*, *sh*, and *th* come together to make one sound. This new sound is called a *digraph*.

Practice

Work with a partner. Take turns.

- Read the sentences.
- Underline the words with *ch*, *sh*, or *th*.
- Circle the letters *ch*, *sh*, or *th* in the words.

1. Living things may change.

2. Fish hatch from eggs.

3. Snakes shed their skin.

4. Silkworms become moths.

101

Informational Text
Science

More About THE BIG QUESTION

Why should people care how animals change as they grow?

Listen to the Audio.

Listen for the general meaning. Think about the situation or context. Use this to help you understand the selection.

Reading Strategy

Recognize Sequence

Recognizing the **sequence**, or order, of events helps you understand the text.

- As you read, pay attention to the order in which events happen.
- Look for words that show sequence, such as *first*, *next*, *then*, and *finally*.

Listen as your teacher models the reading strategy.

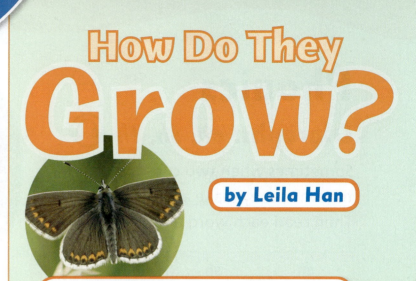

How Do They Grow?

by Leila Han

Learn about how some animals grow and change.

This frog was not always big and brown. This <mark>butterfly</mark> did not always have bright wings.

Living things grow and change. Sometimes the change is **dramatic**, and the living thing experiences a transformation.

Let's look at the transformations that occur in the lives of butterflies and frogs.

_____

dramatic   very noticeable or surprising

Butterfly

First, a butterfly must find a place to lay eggs. A <mark>leaf</mark> is a good place.

Soon an egg will <mark>hatch</mark>, and a tiny <mark>caterpillar</mark> will crawl out. The caterpillar starts to eat right away. It **munches** on plants.

Next, the caterpillar hangs from a branch and builds a chrysalis around itself. It hangs there and does not move. But changes happen inside.

Then the butterfly breaks out of the chrysalis. It spreads its wings and is ready to fly.

---

munches   chews

Before You Go On

What occurs inside the chrysalis?

Frog

Reading Skill

If you don't understand something, ask your classmates or your teacher for help.

A frog lays eggs in the water. Soon, an egg hatches. A tiny tadpole **wiggles** out.

A tadpole lives in the water. It is very **vulnerable**. It must depend on its camouflage to **survive**.

It starts to grow legs. The tadpole's legs grow and grow. Finally, when the tadpole is developed enough, it can leave the water.

___

wiggles   moves from side to side
vulnerable   has no protection
survive   to continue to live

Now the tadpole is a
frog. The frog can hop
on land. It can swim in
the water, too.

WB
102–104

Reading Strategy

Identify Sequence

- What **sequence** words did you find in the selection?
- How does identifying the sequence help you understand the selection?

Think It Over

1. **Recall** Where does a tadpole live?

2. **Comprehend** How does a caterpillar **transform** into a butterfly? Explain.

3. **Analyze** How are the butterfly and the frog similar?

Learning Strategies

Steps in a Process

A **process** is something that happens in order. The parts of a process are called **steps**.

Practice

The list below shows steps that **occur** during a frog's **transformation**. Write a number (1–5) next to each step in the right order.

- The frog hops on land. _____
- The frog lays eggs in the water. _____
- The **tadpole** wiggles out. _____
- The egg **hatches**. _____
- The tadpole grows legs. _____

Use a Sequence Chart

A Sequence Chart can help you put steps in a process in the right order.

Practice
GO 4

This Sequence Chart shows some steps in the life of a <mark>butterfly</mark>.

1. Which step should be in Box 3?
   a. A butterfly comes out of the egg.
   b. A tadpole comes out of the egg.
   c. A <mark>caterpillar</mark> comes out of the egg.
   d. A <mark>chrysalis</mark> comes out of the egg.

2. If there were a Box 6, which step would it be?
   a. The butterfly becomes a caterpillar.
   b. The butterfly spreads its wings.
   c. The butterfly makes a chrysalis.
   d. The butterfly becomes a tadpole.

1. A butterfly lays an egg.
2. The egg hatches.
3.
4. The caterpillar makes a chrysalis. The chrysalis hangs from a branch.
5. A butterfly breaks out of the chrysalis.

105

Apply

Retell the selection to a partner.

Extension

Think of something you do in steps. It can be tying your shoes or brushing your teeth. Make a Sequence Chart. Show the steps you do. Share the chart with your class and explain the steps.

Grammar

Adverbs of Time

An adverb of time tells when an action happened or will happen.

Below are some common adverbs of time.

Adverbs at the end of sentences:

now/today/tomorrow	We should go **now/today/tomorrow**.
early	I left school **early**.
later	I'll see you **later**.
before	I've seen this kind of butterfly **before**.

Adverbs in the middle of sentences:

now	The caterpillar is **now** a butterfly.

Adverbs at the beginning, middle, or end of sentences:

soon	**Soon** the caterpillar will become a butterfly.
	The caterpillar will **soon** become a butterfly.
	The caterpillar will become a butterfly **soon**.

Adverbs of Time and Sequence

Adverbs of time and sequence tell the order, or sequence, in which two or more actions happen.

Step 1	→	**First**, a butterfly lays eggs.
Step 2	→	**Next**, the eggs hatch and a caterpillar crawls out.
Step 3	→	**Then**, the caterpillar builds a chrysalis.
Step 4	→	**Finally**, a butterfly breaks out.

Practice A

Insert the adverbs of time in these sentences. Write the sentences in your notebook.

1. I visited my grandparents. (*yesterday*)
   I visited my grandparents yesterday.

2. I'll be in 4th grade. (*soon*)

3. We'll be home. (*later*)

4. We're in third grade. (*now*)

5. Would you like to see this movie? (*again*)

6. You mix the dry ingredients. (*first*)

7. You put in the wet ingredients. (*then*)

Practice B

Write two sentences in your notebook. Use *soon* and *now* in the middle and at the end of your sentences.

Apply

Work with a partner. Ask and answer the questions. Use adverbs of time in your responses.

Example: A: When do you have lunch?

B: I have lunch soon.

- When do you have art?
- How early do you go to sleep on week nights?
- How soon will you do your homework?
- Are you hungry now?
- Will you go to the library later?

> **Grammar Check ✔**
>
> Name an **adverb of time**. Use it in a sentence.

106

Writing

Write a Personal Narrative

In a personal narrative, you tell about an event or an experience that was important to you.

> ### Writing Prompt
>
> Write a paragraph about an important event in your life. Give details about your experience and explain how you felt. Be sure to use adverbs of time correctly.

① Prewrite

Choose an event to write about. Tell about what happened and how you felt. List your ideas in a Details Chart.

A student named Maki listed her ideas like this:

Event
Losing my first tooth

Detail
I felt my tooth with my tongue. It moved.

Detail
I ran and told my mother.

Detail
It came out the next day.

② Draft

Use your Details Chart to help you write a first draft.
- Keep in mind your purpose—to write a paragraph about a memorable event.
- Include details about what happened and how you felt.

③ Revise

Reread your draft. Look for places where it needs improvement. Use the Writing Checklist to help you find problems. Then revise your draft.

④ Edit

Check your work for errors. Do Peer Review (use the Checklist on page 402).

⑤ Publish

Make a clean copy of your final draft. Share it with the class. Save your work for the Writing Workshop.

Here is Maki's story:

Writing Checklist

✓ **Ideas**
I included important details about what happened.
I expressed my ideas clearly.

✓ **Conventions**
I used adverbs of time correctly.
I used the past tense correctly.

Maki Umamoto

The Day I Lost My First Tooth

   I am six years old. I lost my first baby tooth yesterday. I felt the tooth loosen. I moved it with my tongue. I ran and showed my mother. The next day, I put my tongue where my loose tooth was. I knew that it will fall out soon. Later that day, I was eating a sandwich. I felt for my loose tooth again, but it was gone! My mother and I looked everywhere for it. Finally, I found it. It was in my sandwich!

107–108

Apply and Extend

Link the Readings

Look at the chart. Read the words in the top row.

- For *Animal Habitats / Alligators and Crocodiles*, put an X under the words that remind you of the poems.

- Repeat the same activity for the other readings.

	Informational text	Literature	Survival	Habitat / environment
Animal Habitats / Alligators and Crocodiles				
Can You See Them?				
How Do They Grow?				

Discussion

1. What animals do the two poems talk about?

2. How do some animals camouflage themselves in their **environment**? Why do they do it?

3. What changes **occur** when butterflies and frogs begin to **transform**?

 What can we learn about animals and why is learning about them important?

Listening Skills

If you can't hear someone, you can say, "Could you speak more loudly, please?"

Projects

Your teacher will help you choose one of these projects.

Written	Oral	Visual/Active
Animal Facts Choose an animal that you like. Write three facts about it. Tell where it lives, what it eats, and what it looks like.	**Guessing Game** Make a list of facts about an animal. Tell what it eats and where it lives. Have a partner guess the animal.	**Diorama** Make a diorama. Show sky, land, and water. Show where animals live. Share your diorama with the class.
Animal Story Write a story about an animal. Tell about its home. Tell how the animal found its home.	**Talk About It** Find out about an animal that uses camouflage to stay safe. Give a formal presentation about the animal to your class.	**Habitat Mobile** Make a mobile. Show pictures of animals in their homes. Write a fact on the back of each picture.

For more resources, visit **Pearson English Portal**.

WB
109–110

Listening and Speaking Workshop

Recite a Poem

You are going to write and recite a poem. Then you will listen as your classmates recite their poems.

① Prepare

A. Choose a favorite activity or animal. You will write a poem about it and recite it to the class. Your classmates will tell you how your poem makes them feel.

B. Recall what you know about your favorite activity or animal. Then write your poem about it.

Useful Language

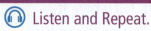 Listen and Repeat.

I'm going to recite a poem.
My poem is about...
I wrote it myself.
Ready?...
How did my poem make you feel?

> One day,
> Eating a leaf, all green and new.
> One day,
> Looking at the sky, all big and blue.
> One day,
> Going to fly, all pretty like you!

② Practice

Practice your poem until you have memorized it. Practice in front of your family or friends. If possible, record your presentation. Then listen to yourself. How do you sound? Record yourself again and try to improve.

③ Present

As you speak, do the following:

- Speak clearly and with feeling.

- If you forget a word, don't worry! Just go on with your poem.

- After your poem, ask your classmates how it made them feel.

As you listen, do the following:

- Listen to how your classmate speaks with feeling and expression.

- Listen carefully for ideas and information that is implied, or not stated directly.

- Write down any new words you hear.

Speaking Skills

Poems use informal language. It is OK to use single words, short phrases, or incomplete sentences to express your thoughts and feelings.

Listening Skills

Watch and listen carefully. Give the speaker your full attention.

④ Evaluate

After you speak, answer these questions:

✔ Did you memorize your poem?

✔ Did you speak with feeling?

After you listen, answer these questions:

✔ What was the poem about?

✔ How did the poem make you feel?

✔ Think about the general meaning of the poem. Can you think of a title for it? Tell your idea to the class.

Writing Workshop
Write a Personal Narrative

Writing Prompt

Write a personal narrative. Give details about something you experienced.
Say why the experience was important to you and what you learned from it.
Speak directly to the reader. Be sure your narrative has a beginning, a middle,
and an end.

① Prewrite

Review the writing you have done in this unit. Then choose something
that happened to you to write about. List the details in a chart.

A student named May listed her ideas like this:

Event	Going to music camp
When	Last summer
Where	by a lake
Details	1. My mom said I should go to music camp
	2. My last experience at a camp was not good.
	3. I loved the music camp.
How It Ended	I learned to give things a chance.

② Draft

Use your chart to help you write a first draft.

- Keep in mind your purpose—to write a personal narrative.

- Include why it was important or what you learned from it.

③ Revise

Read your draft. Look for places where the writing needs improvement. Use the Writing Checklist to help you find problems. Then revise your draft.

Here is how May revised her essay:

Six Traits of Writing Checklist

✔ **Ideas**
Did I say why the experience was important to me?

✔ **Organization**
Did my narrative have a beginning, middle, and end?

✔ **Voice**
Did I speak directly to the reader?

✔ **Words**
Did I use words that will keep my readers interested?

✔ **Sentence Fluency**
Did I use different kinds of sentences?

✔ **Conventions**
Did I use negative forms correctly?

May Yang

Music Camp

    ~~This~~ ^{Last} summer my mom sent me to music camp. I really didn't want to go. Why?

    Two summers ago I went to a summer camp. I hated it. The counselors ~~are~~ ^{were} strict and the kids weren't nice. I didn't have fun.

    But this camp was different. The kids were ^{very} ᐱ nice. The counselors weren't too strict. I was playing my guitar all day and doing other fun activities. I really enjoyed the rest of my time ~~in~~ ^{at} the camp.

    I learned from this experience that I shouldn't decide about things before I do them. I have to give things a chance.

> **Revised** to correct adverb of time.

> **Revised** to correct verb tense.

> **Revised** to add adverb for emphasis.

> **Revised** to correct use of preposition.

④ Edit

Check your work for errors. Trade papers with a partner to get feedback. Use the Peer Review Checklist.

⑤ Publish

Make a clean copy of your final draft. Share it with the class.

111–112

Peer Review Checklist

✔ Events are told in a logical order.

✔ All the information is related to the topic.

✔ The narrative includes interesting details.

Spelling Tip

A contraction consists of two words that are joined and shortened by replacing a letter or letters with an apostrophe (').
Form a negative contraction with a verb + n't (an apostrophe replaces the o in *not*).
For example *were + not = weren't*.

Fluency

Listen to the sentences. Pay attention to the groups of words. Read aloud.

1. Animals share the world with us, as pets or wild and free.

2. Some animals use camouflage to be safe from predators.

3. Living things such as frogs and butterflies change as they grow.

Work in pairs. Take turns reading aloud the passage below for one minute. Count the number of words you read.

How Do They Grow? tells how a butterfly and a frog	11
grow and change over their lifetimes. The butterfly starts	20
as an egg, which then hatches to become a caterpillar. The	31
caterpillar surrounds itself in a chrysalis and later changes	40
into a butterfly.	43
The frog also starts life as an egg, which then hatches to	55
become a little tadpole. Over time, the tadpole grows legs	65
and then moves from the water onto land. It is now a frog.	78
It can hop on land and swim in the water, too.	89

With your partner, find the words that slowed you down.

- Practice saying each word and then say the sentence each word is in.

- Then take turns reading the text again. Count the number of words you read.

WB
113

Taking Tests

You will often take tests that help show what you know. Follow these tips to improve your test-taking skills.

Coaching Corner

Answering Test Questions That Are Cloze Items

- A cloze passage is a reading selection that has blanks for you to fill in. Each blank will have a number. Then you will be given answer choices for each number. You need to choose which of the choices is best to complete the numbered blank in the passage.

- Remember to pay attention to the words and sentences before and after each blank in the passage. You will often find clues in the selection that will help you choose the best word to fill in the blank.

- After you read all the answer choices, think of each word in the blank and read the sentence aloud each time. Reading the sentence aloud will help you choose the word that makes the most sense.

W B
115–116

Read the selection. Then choose the correct words to fill in the blanks.

The Traveling Tank

1   An armadillo is a small __1__ whose back, head, legs, and tail are covered with bony plates of "armor." The name "armadillo" is a Spanish word that means "little armored one." These bands of armor give protection to the armadillo. If an armadillo feels unsafe, it will curl up into a ball until the danger is gone.

2   Armadillos have small eyes. They cannot see very well. Instead, they rely on their __2__ sense of smell to hunt. An armadillo uses its sharp __3__ and strong legs to dig for food. It uses its pointy snout and long, sticky tongue to find and eat all sorts of insects.

1 **A** flower

   B mammal

   C fish

   D tree

2 **F** weak

   G colorful

   H small

   J strong

3 **A** feet

   B face

   C claws

   D armor

Tips

✓ Read the whole selection before you try to fill in the blanks. This will give you a better idea of what information is missing.

✓ Use the information in the passage to create a picture of an armadillo in your head. Use this picture to help you answer the questions.

Great Ideas

Create art. Explore in science. Start with an idea and build on it. That's how we get great ideas.

Reading 1
Article

On Your Bike, Get Set, Donate!

Reading 2
Science

Scientists and Crows

Reading 3
Photo Essay

Accidental Inventions

THE BiG QUESTION

What are some great ideas that make our world a better place?

Listening and Speaking

You will talk about great ideas and inventions. In the Listening and Speaking Workshop, you will give a presentation.

Writing

You will practice expository writing. In the Writing Workshop, you will write to compare and contrast.

Quick Write

People can have great ideas in science and art. Make a list of other areas people can have great ideas in.

View and Respond

Talk about the poster for this unit. Then watch and listen to the video and answer the questions at Pearson English Portal.

What do you know about people with great ideas?

Words to Know

Listen and repeat. Talk about these people with great ideas.

inventor

actor

writer

builder

painter

gardener

Practice

Work with a partner. Ask and answer questions.

act in plays and movies	build houses	grow plants
paint pictures	write books	invent things

Example: A: What do <u>actors</u> do? B: They <u>act in plays</u>.

Write

Choose a job from above. Write sentences in your notebook.

Make Connections

Read each sentence. Write your answer in the blank.

plays

paintings

stories

gardens

inventions

buildings

1. Builders create these. They come in many different sizes.

_____

2. The students at my school love to act. We create these during the school year. _____

3. My mom creates these in our backyard with flowers and vegetables. _____

4. I create these in art class. I use paints and brushes. _____

5. Writers create these so we can read or hear them. _____

6. Scientists create these. Sometimes it takes years and years to finish them. _____

What about you?

Talk with a partner. What do you like to create? What can your parents and brothers or sisters create?

Build Unit Background

Kids' Stories from around the World

 England

France

U.S.A.

Allison

Most plants grow in dirt. In my school in Vermont, U.S.A., we are learning how to grow plants in water. We put food for the plants in the water. Scientists have grown plants this way. This can help countries that don't have much land. Farmers can use water to help them grow more food.

Colin

I am a reporter in England even though I am nine years old! I am part of a news group that is run by young people. We decide what to write about. Then we talk with people. Our stories are in newspapers, on websites, and on the radio.

Azerbaijan

Zarifa

I live in Azerbaijan. We have a museum of tiny books. There are more than 4,000 books. The biggest book is only 4 inches tall! A woman who loves books opened this museum.

Anton

Many people in my country, France, love to ski. Some schools in France teach people who are physically challenged how to ski. These people can take part in special races, too. This way, everyone can have fun in the snow!

What about you?

1. What is your great idea? (Remember, sometimes a great idea can be small.)

2. Do you have a story about someone else's great idea? Share your story.

Key Words

On Your Bike, Get Set, Donate! is about organizations that fix old bicycles to give to people who need them.

Words in Context

1 Each year, my school holds a Read-a-thon. Parents **donate** children's books. **Volunteers** from my school sign up to read up to 10 books in one month.

What You Will Learn

Reading

- Vocabulary building: *Context, word study*
- Reading strategy: *Identify problems and solutions*
- Text type: Informational text *(magazine article)*

Grammar

need/want/like/love + to + verb

Writing

Describe a problem and solution

These words will help you understand the reading.

Key Words

donate

volunteers

bicycles

helmets

2 **Bicycles** are also called bikes. A bicycle has two wheels.

3 These kids are wearing safety **helmets**.

Practice

Make flashcards to help you memorize the words.

• Write a key word on the front.
• On the back, write the meaning.

Make Connections

How can you ride a bicycle safely? What should you wear? Where should you ride? Use some of the key words as you speak.

These words will help you talk about the reading.

Academic Words

benefit
helped by

normally
most of the time

Academic Words

Words in Context

Our bodies **benefit** from eating healthy food. It gives us more energy.

The children **normally** walk to school, but today they can ride their new bikes.

Practice

Use an academic word to complete each sentence.

1. We _____ from getting 8 or 9 hours of sleep every night. It helps our memory.

2. The post office is _____ open on Mondays, but today it is closed. It is a holiday.

Apply

Ask and answer with a partner.

1. Sometimes we make mistakes, like forgetting to bring our homework to school. How can we **benefit** from our mistakes? Give an example.

2. What do you **normally** do on Saturdays? What about last Saturday? Was it a typical Saturday?

118

Word Study

Pronunciation of Ending -ed

Listen. Then read aloud.

> The children **started** school.
> The boys **repaired** the bike.

The words *started* and *repaired* both tell about the past. But the ending -ed is pronounced differently in each word.

> start + ed = start/ed   repair + ed = repaired

Rule

> Look for this pattern in English: if the letter *d* or the letter *t* comes before the -ed ending, then -ed is pronounced as a separate syllable.

Practice

Work with a partner. Take turns.

- Sound out the words in the box.
- Add -ed to each word. Read the new word aloud.
- Tell if the -ed adds a syllable to the word.

1. add
2. help
3. seat
4. play
5. show

119

Informational Text
Magazine Article

More About THE BiG QUESTION

How can people use a great idea to help others?

🎧 **Listen to the Audio.**
Listen for the main points and important details.

Reading Strategy

Identify Problems and Solutions

Identifying problems and solutions helps you understand a text better. To identify problems and solutions, follow these steps:

- What problems are described?
- What are the solutions, and who helps find them?

Listen as your teacher models the reading strategy.

On Your Bike, Get Set, Donate!

by Jamaila Veglia

People like to ride bicycles. Every year, many people buy new bicycles. What happens to the old **bikes**? People throw away many of them. What a waste!

----

bikes   bicycles

These boys can fix bikes.

A Great Idea

Bicycle riders can donate their old bikes to groups of people who have a great idea. These groups **fix** the bikes. Then the groups give the bikes to children who don't have bicycles. The groups may give bikes to grown-ups who need them, too. Some groups send bicycles to people in other countries.

―――――――――――――――

fix   make like new

Groups fix bikes and give them to people who need them.

Before You Go On

In many parts of the world, what **normally** happens to old bikes?

Kids get helmets, too!

A volunteer works to repair a bike.

Volunteers Help

Bicycle Exchange is a group that gives away bikes. Each year, people donate their old bikes to this group. People in Bicycle Exchange teach <mark>volunteers</mark> how to fix bikes. Then, the volunteers work to **repair** old bikes. At the end of the year, Bicycle Exchange gives bikes to children. The group also gives <mark>helmets</mark> to children. People in the group teach children bicycle safety, too. Children need to know how to ride and be safe.

---

repair fix

It can be fun to fix old bikes.

A Boy Helps Others

Young people can help, too. Joshua started fixing bikes when he was twelve years old. He gave them to children who did not have bicycles.

Joshua got started when his own bike broke. He had an idea. He would learn how to fix it himself. Soon, neighbors were bringing old bikes to Joshua's house. He repaired them. Now other children have new bikes.

Young people can help.

Before You Go On

What was Joshua's idea? How did others **benefit** from his idea?

Around the World

Groups send bicycles to countries where it is not easy to buy a bike. One group, Cyclo Nord-Sud, sent 400 bikes to Togo. Many children must walk ten miles or more to get to school in Togo. Bikes can really help!

Another group, Bike Works, sends bikes to **villages** in Ghana. Farmers, teachers, and students use the bikes to get to work and to school.

---

villages   very small towns in the country

Reading Skill

The word **ten** is a basic sight word. The more you read, the more words you will recognize automatically.

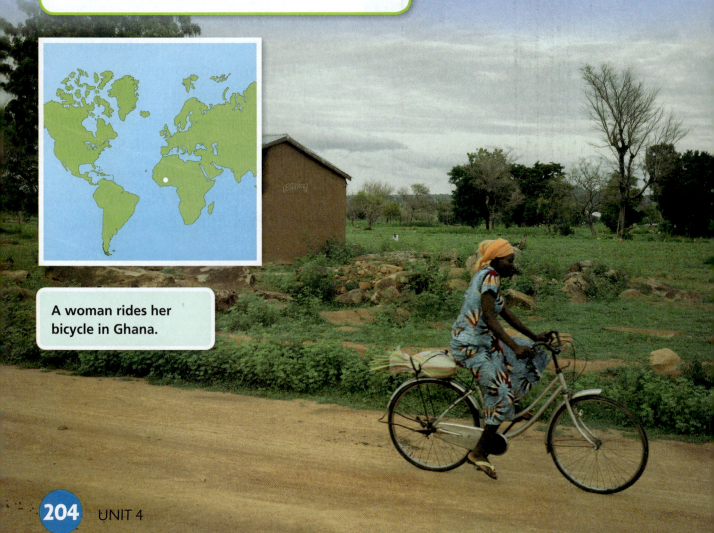

A woman rides her bicycle in Ghana.

Riders Write Back

Volunteers love to hear from new bike riders. They like to know that their work makes people happy.

A group called Second Chance got a poem from one rider.

Bike Works got a note from a young girl in Ghana. "I love my bike," she wrote. "It is blue which is my **favorite** color."

---

favorite   one you like best

Bikes are tight.

They make me

Feel all right.

I love my bike.
It is blue, which is
my favorite color.
Lakiska

W B
120–122

Think It Over

1. **Recall** How does Bicycle Exchange help people?

2. **Comprehend** What do Joshua and the other groups in this selection have in common?

3. **Analyze** Why is it a waste to throw away an old bicycle?

Bicycles

▲ Tricycle

A tricycle has three wheels. Small children can ride tricycles.

Unicycle ▲

It takes a lot of practice to ride this unicycle! Do you think you could ride it?

▲ High-Wheel Bicycle

The high-wheel <mark>bicycle</mark> was first made in 1871. Riders cannot put their feet on the ground. How do you think that would feel?

Delivery Bike ▲

A rider could use this bike to take packages to people.

▲ BMX Bikes

These girls race on BMX bikes. Riders can do tricks and ride on dirt roads with these bikes.

Mountain Bike ▶

This man is riding a mountain bike. These bikes go on dirt trails or bumpy roads. They have wide tires.

▲ Wheelchair Cycle

This man can ride or race on this wheelchair cycle.

Activity to Do

These two pages use words and pictures to tell about bicycles.

- Choose another machine used for travel.

- Find pictures to show that machine.

- Post your pictures with captions in your classroom.

Learning Strategies
Problems and Solutions

A magazine article can tell how people find solutions to problems.

Practice

Read these sentences about the selection. Tell which sentences are problems. Tell which sentences are solutions.

1. Many people throw away old bikes.
2. Many children do not have bicycles.
3. Bicycle Exchange volunteers teach people how to fix old bikes.
4. Groups give repaired bicycles to people who need them.
5. In many countries, it is not easy to buy a bike.

Use a T-Chart

You can use a T-Chart to help you understand the selection.

GO 9

Practice

Use the steps below to see how each group or person solved the problems in the selection. Write your responses in the chart.

Group or Person	Solution
Bicycle Exchange	_____ _____
Joshua	_____ _____
_____	_____ _____

- List two or more things Bicycle Exchange does to solve the problems.
- List two or more things Joshua does to solve the problems.
- List one more group. Tell one thing the group does to solve the problems.

Apply

Summarize the selection for a partner. Use some of the key words.

123

Extension

Choose one thing that you could give away. Draw a picture of it. Write about why someone else might want it. Present your idea to the class.

Grammar

Need/Want + to + Verb

Need and *want* are always followed by *to* + verb
(called an *infinitive*).

> It **needs to be delivered** today.
> He **needs to study** right now.
> They **want to fix** your bike.

Like/Love + to + Verb

Like and **love** can also be followed by *to* + verb.

> She **likes to bike** to school.
> We **love to watch** you race.

To make negative sentences with *need* and *want* in the
present tense, use *do* or *does not* + *need* or *want* + *to* +
verb (infinitive).

Affirmative	Negative
She **needs** to buy it. ⟶	She **does not need** to buy it.
	She **doesn't need** to buy it.
I **want** to donate it. ⟶	I **do not want** to donate it.
	I **don't want** to donate it.

Practice A

Complete the sentences with *to* + verb.
Use words from the box.

donate	answer	wear	close	finish	ride

1. My little brother likes ___to answer___ the phone.

2. He needs _____ a <mark>helmet</mark> when he rides.

3. We want _____ the window.

4. They love _____ their new skateboards.

5. I need _____ my homework.

6. She wants _____ her bike to someone in need.

Practice B

Make the sentences in Practice A negative. Write the sentences in your notebook.

Apply

Work with a partner. Ask and answer the questions.
Use *to* + verb in your answers.

Example: A: What do you want to do after school?

B: I want to play baseball after school.

- Do you like to listen to music?
- Do you need to finish your homework?
- Where do you like to go on the weekend?
- What shows do you love to watch on TV?
- What games do you like to play?

124

Writing

Describe a Problem and Solution

Expository writing is writing that gives information or explains something. One example of expository writing is a problem and solution paragraph.

Writing Prompt

Write about a problem you or someone you know had and how it was solved. Be sure to use verb + *to* + infinitive correctly.

① Prewrite

GO 9

Choose a situation to write about. Tell about what the problem was and how it was solved. List your ideas in a T-chart.

A student named Aiza Lee listed her ideas like this:

PROBLEM	SOLUTION
I lost my backpack.	My friend helped me. He asked me to think when I last had it. I thought about it, and then I remembered. I had it in my karate class.

② Draft

Use your T-chart to help you write a first draft.

- Keep in mind your purpose—to describe a problem and how it was solved.
- Include details about what the problem was and how it was solved.

③ Revise

Reread your draft. Look for places where it needs improvement. Use the Writing Checklist to help you find problems. Then revise your draft.

④ Edit

Check your work for errors. Use the Peer Review Checklist on page 402.

⑤ Publish

Make a clean copy of your final draft. Share it with the class. Save your work for the Writing Workshop.

Here is Aiza Lee's story about her problem:

Aiza Lee

Last week, I lost my red backpack. I looked at home and at school. I needed to find it before the weekend. I had to study for two big tests. My friend Aidan wanted to help me. He asked me, "When did you last have it? What did you do? Where did you go?" I thought and thought. Then I remembered. I had it when I went to my karate class. Maybe I left it there! I went to the karate classroom. There was my red backpack. I was so happy!

Writing Checklist

✓ **Ideas**
I described the problem and the solution.

I expressed my ideas clearly.

✓ **Conventions**
I used verb + *to* + verb correctly.

I used the past tense correctly.

The subjects and verbs in my sentences agree.

WB
125–126

Key Words

In *Scientists and Crows,* you will read about how scientists study crows.

Words in Context

1 Babies cry when they are hungry or tired. They cry to show they need help. No one teaches babies how to cry. They know by **instinct**.

2 How do I know the kitten took the toy bird? This photo is the **proof**.

3 A rake is a **tool** that people use in a garden.

4 Jane Goodall is a <mark>scientist</mark>. She studies chimpanzees in their habitat.

5 This scientist works in a <mark>lab</mark>.

Practice

Make flashcards to help you memorize the words.

- Write a key word on the front.
- On the back, write a sentence, but leave a blank where the key word should be.

Make Connections

Do you know of a smart animal? What can this animal do? Tell the class about it.

These words will help you talk about the reading.

Academic Words

method
a way of doing something

theory
unproven idea that explains something

Academic Words

Words in Context

My **method** for learning new words is to write them in my vocabulary notebook.

Can plants grow without sunlight? Our **theory** is they can't. We'll do an experiment to find out.

Practice

Use an academic word to complete each sentence.

1. The scientist has a _____ that explains why more people get sick in the winter.

2. Our dad uses a special _____ to wake us up in the morning. He turns the light in our room on and off several times.

Apply

Ask and answer with a partner.

1. How do you study for exams? Do you study alone or with friends? Talk about what **method** works best for you.

2. Why do people smile when they are happy? Think of a **theory** that could explain this.

128

Phonics

R-Controlled Vowels: *ir, er, ur*

The letter *r* after a vowel gives the vowel a new sound. Listen. Then read each word aloud.

b**i**d	g**e**m	h**u**t
b**i**rd	g**e**rm	h**u**rt

Rule

The letters *ir*, *er*, and *ur* usually have the same vowel sound.

Practice

Work with a partner.

- Sort the words in the box into three lists:
    words with *ir*
    words with *er*
    words with *ur*
- Sound out the words in your lists.
- Add a new word to each list.

dirt	curb	herd
fern	her	perch
first	hurt	third
fur	girl	turn

Informational Text
Science

More About THE BiG QUESTION

How can people try out their ideas to learn new things?

🎧 **Listen to the Audio.**
Listen for the main points and important details.

Reading Strategy

Identify Main Idea and Details

The main idea is the most important idea in a selection. Details are the facts or pieces of information that support or explain the main idea.

- As you read, look for the main idea of the selection.
- Look for details that tell about the main idea.

Listen as your teacher models the reading strategy.

Scientists and Crows

by Remore Williams
illustrated by Laura Jacobsen

Do you ever watch crows? You may see crows fly over trees. You may see a crow sit on a power line. Maybe you hear crows call, "Caw! Caw! Caw!"

Scientists watch crows, too. They watch what crows do in their habitat. They also study crows in labs. Scientists study crows to learn more about them.

Crows and Clams

Crows eat clams. Clams are small animals that live inside a **shell**. The shell is hard. How can a crow eat an animal inside a shell? Some scientists in Japan studied some crows to find out.

The scientists watched crows eating clams. The crows picked up the clams with their beaks. They carried the clams high in the air, and then dropped them to the ground. When the shells hit the ground, they broke. Then the crows ate the clams.

---

shell   hard outer part

Before You Go On

What method did the crows use to open clams?

Crows and Walnuts

Crows eat walnuts, too. Walnuts are **nuts** that have very hard shells. How can a crow break the shell? The scientists learned by watching this, too.

Some crows dropped walnuts on a street. Cars drove over the shells and **cracked** them. Then the crows ate the nuts.

Sometimes a crow did not drop the walnuts. Sometimes a crow carried a walnut, put it down in a **crosswalk**, and flew away. Cars drove over the walnut and cracked the shell. Then the crow came back and ate the walnut.

---

nuts   dry fruit inside shells

cracked   broke the outside part to get what was inside

crosswalk   a marked place to cross a street

Scientists know that birds do many things by instinct. For example, they learn to fly by instinct. But the crows in Japan seemed to be solving a problem. How could the scientists find out if the crows were using instinct or solving a problem?

The scientists had a great idea. They would test crows in a lab. They would try to learn if a crow could solve a problem. They would find the proof.

Before You Go On

What methods did the crows use to open walnuts?

Crows in a Lab

The scientists gave the crows this problem. They put food in a tiny bucket with a handle. The bucket was at the bottom of a tube. The crows could not reach the bucket without using a tool .

Scientists gave the crows two wires. One wire was straight. The other wire was bent, like a hook. A crow could lift the bucket with the bent wire.

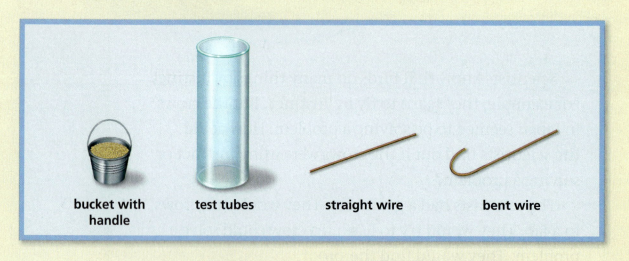

bucket with handle   test tubes   straight wire   bent wire

A crow named Betty used the bent wire to lift the bucket four times.

Then, the scientists took away the bent wire. Betty tried to use the straight wire to lift the bucket. It didn't work. Betty needed a hook.

Then, Betty bent the wire herself. She lifted the bucket out of the tube with her new tool. Betty had made the right tool for the job!

Scientists learned that Betty the crow could solve a problem. This is not proof that all crows can solve problems. Scientists have to do more tests. They have to study other crows. But scientists used a great idea to learn something new about crows.

This crow waits to find insects to eat.

130–132

Reading Strategy

Identify Main Ideas and Details

- What is the main idea?
- What details tell about the main idea?
- How did looking for the main idea help you understand the selection?

Think It Over

1. **Recall** What did Betty the crow do in the lab?

2. **Comprehend** What theory were scientists testing in the lab?

3. **Analyze** Some crows dropped walnuts in the street. Betty bent a wire. What do these two actions have in common?

Learning Strategies

Main Idea and Details

The **main idea** is the most important idea in a selection.
Details give important information to support the main
idea. **Support** means to help show something is true.

Practice

Read these sentences about the selection.

- Tell which one is the main idea.
- Tell which ones are details that support the main idea.

1. Crows crack walnuts by putting them in the street.
2. Crows break clams by dropping them on the ground.
3. Scientists study crows in their habitat and in labs.
4. In a lab, a crow bent a wire to get food.

Use a Main Idea and Details Chart

This chart can help you figure out the main idea of the selection. You can show the details that support the main idea.

Practice
GO 1

Fill in the main idea and details.

- What is the main idea of *Scientists and Crows*?
- Reread the selection. Find three details that support the main idea.

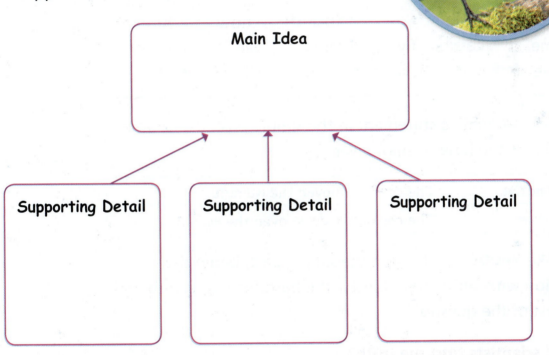

Main Idea

Supporting Detail

Supporting Detail

Supporting Detail

W B
133

Apply

Reread the selection and take notes. Then close your book and summarize the selection for a partner.

Extension

What animal would you like to study? What would you like to learn about the animal? Talk with a partner about how you would find out more about that animal.

Grammar

Simple Past: Irregular Verbs

Some verbs have an irregular simple past form.

Simple Present	Simple Past
Crows **eat** the nuts. ⟶	The crows **ate** the nuts in the crosswalk.

Review these **common irregular verbs** from the reading.

break ⟶ **broke**	find ⟶ **found**	know ⟶ **knew**
come ⟶ **came**	fly ⟶ **flew**	see ⟶ **saw**
drive ⟶ **drove**	give ⟶ **gave**	sit ⟶ **sat**

To make a negative statement in the simple past, use **did not** or **didn't** + the base form of a verb.

Affirmative	The car **drove** over the walnuts.
Negative	The car **didn't drive** over the walnuts.

To make *Yes/No* questions in the simple past, begin the question with **Did** + the subject + the base form of a verb and the rest of the question.

Did scientists **find** the truth?

To make *Wh-* questions, begin the question with a question word (for example, *What, Where, When*) + *did* + *subject* + *verb* and the rest of the question.

What did the crow **do** with the clams, so it could eat them?
Where did it **put the** walnuts before it flew away?

Practice A

Change each irregular verb to the past form. Write the sentences.

1. The crows ~~sit~~ ^sat^ on the power line.

2. The clams break on the ground.

3. The crow flies away.

4. People give crows food.

5. A scientist takes the <mark>tool</mark> from Betty.

6. Scientists see Betty solve the problem.

Practice B

Change the sentences in Practice A into negative sentences. Share them aloud with a partner.

Apply

Work with a partner. Ask and answer the questions. Use irregular simple past verbs in your answers.

Example: A: Did you already eat breakfast?

B: Yes, I ate breakfast at 6:45.

134

- Did you break your pencil last week?
- Did you already know your teacher on the first day of school?
- Did you give someone a present last month?
- Where did you find something you lost?

Grammar Check ✔

Name some **irregular verbs** and their past form.

Writing
Respond to Text

After you read a text, you can write a response. In a response, you say what you think about the text.

Writing Prompt

Write your response to the text *Scientists and Crows*. Be sure to use the simple past of irregular verbs correctly.

① Prewrite GO 12

Think about the selection *Scientists and Crows*. Complete a chart with what you knew before you read the article, what you found interesting about it, and what surprised you. List your ideas in a three-column chart.

A student named Christina listed her ideas like this:

Crows		
What I Knew	**What I Found Interesting**	**What I Learned That Surprised Me**
Crows break things apart with their beaks.	Crows figure out ways to break things open.	Crows figured out how to make hooks.

② Draft

Use your three-column chart to help you write a first draft.

- Keep in mind your purpose—to write your response to the text.
- Include what you found interesting and what you learned.

3 Revise

Reread your draft. Look for places where it needs improvement. Use the Writing Checklist to help you find problems. Then revise your draft.

4 Edit

Check your work for errors. Use the Peer Review Checklist on page 402.

5 Publish

Make a clean copy of your final draft. Share it with the class. Save your work. You will need it for the Writing Workshop.

Here is Christina's reaction to the text:

Writing Checklist

✔ **Ideas**
I included what interested me about the text and what surprised me.
I expressed my ideas clearly.

✔ **Conventions**
I used the simple past of irregular verbs correctly.
The nouns and pronouns in my sentences agree.

Christina Ramos

I thought the article <u>Scientists and Crows</u> was very interesting. I knew that crows could break things apart with their sharp beaks, but I didn't know they could break apart things in different ways. For example, they fly high and drop things in the street so cars will break them apart. It surprised me that the crows in the experiment in Japan bent the wire into hooks so they could get the food. Amazing!

WB
135–136

Key Words

In *Accidental Inventions*, you will learn about some things that were invented by accident.

Words in Context

What You Will Learn

Reading
- Vocabulary building: *Context, phonics*
- Reading strategy: *Ask questions*
- Text type: *Informational text (photo essay)*

Grammar
Nouns: common and proper

Writing
Explain a process

These words will help you understand the reading.

Key Words

Key Words
invented
creation
solve
accident
discover

1 Alexander Graham Bell **invented** the telephone.

2 Sarah showed her **creation** to the class.

3 Charlotte helped Ben **solve** the math problem.

4 Lee spilled his water by <mark>accident</mark>.

5 You <mark>discover</mark> new things when you explore.

Practice

Draw pictures of the key words in your notebook. Label the pictures using sentences that contain the key words.

Make Connections

Have you ever done something by accident? Describe what happened. Do you think accidents are always a bad thing, or could something good happen by accident? Explain your answer.

These words will help you talk about the reading.

Academic Words

imply
say something in an indirect way

symbol
something that stands for an idea

Academic Words

Words in Context

My teacher told us to review the chapter this weekend. I think he was trying to **imply** there will be a test on Monday.

She uses the sun in her paintings as a **symbol** of happiness.

Practice

Choose an academic word to complete each sentence.

1. The bald eagle is a _____ of freedom in the United States.

2. She talks a lot about nature in her poetry. Her words _____ she cares about Earth.

Apply

Ask and answer with a partner.

1. What is a **symbol** of happiness to you?

2. What words can you use to **imply** that you like something, without using the word *like*?

WB
138

Phonics

Hard and Soft c

A **hard c** sounds like the *k* in *kite*. *Classroom* has a **hard c**.

A **soft c** sounds like the *s* in *sun*. *Center* has a **soft c**.

My seat is in the **center** of my **classroom**.

Rule

The letter *c* is soft when it is followed by *e*, *i*, or *y*.
The letter *c* is hard when followed by *a*, *o*, or *u*.

Practice

Work with a partner. Take turns.

- Read the sentences aloud.
- List the words with a soft *c* sound.
- List the words with a hard *c* sound.

1. Did you notice how many calls you got on your cell phone?

2. Once, the cold froze the water in my cup.

3. A scientist came to speak to our class.

4. My computer fell and broke into several pieces.

More About THE **BiG** QUESTION ?

How do the things people make show their ideas?

🎧 **Listen to the Audio.**
Listen for the main points and important details.

Reading Strategy

Ask Questions

As you read, ask yourself questions to make sure you understand what you are reading.

- Read the captions and look at the photographs.
- Ask yourself what story each object tells.

Listen as your teacher models the reading strategy.

Accidental Inventions

by Katie Harper

Look around at the things you use each day. You probably see computers, cell phones, toys, tools, and more. At one time, each of these did not exist. They all came about because someone **invented** them.

An invention is a useful **creation**. Most inventions begin as an idea. Someone sees a need or a problem. Then he or she thinks of an idea to meet that need or **solve** the problem.

Not all inventions happen on purpose. Sometimes people invent something by **accident**. They may be working on an idea and accidentally invent something else. Or an inventor might make a mistake that turns out to be a good idea.

You might be surprised to learn which things started out as accidental inventions.

In 1905, a boy named Frank Epperson left a cup of soda outside all night. It had a wooden stirring stick in it. Overnight, the air turned cold. The soda froze. In the morning, Frank took a lick of the frozen treat. It tasted really good! He called his accidental invention the "Episicle." He shared the frozen soda with his friends and, years later, with his children, too. They told him to change the name to what they called it: Pop's 'Sicle, or Popsicle®.

Between AD 600 and 900, scientists in China were working in a lab when they accidentally invented fireworks. The story is that they were working on an invention that would help people live forever. They mixed together ingredients like salt, charcoal, and sulfur. These were all common in kitchens back then. They put the mixture into pieces of **bamboo**. Then they tossed them into a fire. BOOM!

bamboo   a tropical plant with tall, hollow stems

Before You Go On

The original name of the Popsicle was Episicle. What is the name a **symbol** of?

In 1968, scientist Spencer Silver was researching **adhesives** when he <mark>discovered</mark> one that stuck to things, but could then be easily removed. For years he tried to find a use for his invention. At the same time, another scientist named Art Fry sang in a **choir**. He used small pieces of paper to mark the songs in his songbook. But they always fell out. He needed bookmarks that would stay in place. Silver and Fry discussed their ideas and created the Post-it® Note.

---

adhesive   a substance that is used to make things stick firmly together

choir   a group of people who sing together

In 1948, George de Mestral was hiking with his dog. As they walked, he noticed **cockleburs** sticking to his pants and his dog's fur. He wondered how they were able to stick so well. He decided to take a few of the cockleburs to examine under a **microscope**. He saw that the cockleburs had tiny hooks that stuck to his pants. He then figured out a way to copy the hook and loop. His invention became Velcro® Brand Fasteners.

---

cocklebur   a plant that has tiny hooks that stick to things

microscope   a scientific tool that makes very small things look bigger

Many toys have been invented by accident, including Play-Doh, Silly Putty, and the Slinky.

Play-Doh® was once used to clean wallpaper. Then Joe McVicker learned from a teacher that her students had a hard time using modeling clay. He discovered that the wallpaper cleaner he used was a good **substitute** for the clay. He sent some to the school, and soon sent some to other schools, too. By 1956 the cleaner became Play-Doh. Children have been playing with it ever since.

substitute   something that takes the place of something else

During World War II, James Wright was making a new kind of rubber for the U.S. government. He came up with something that stretched and bounced better than rubber. But the government did not like his "nutty putty." But a businessman did. He saw it at a party. He noticed how much fun children had with it. He named it Silly Putty®!

In 1943 Richard James was trying to make a spring to use on ships. One day one of his springs fell off a shelf. He watched in amazement as the spring "walked" down the shelves. He and his wife turned the springs into toys for kids. They named their accidental invention the Slinky®!

140–142

Think It Over

1. **Recall** Name three accidental inventions you read about in the article.

2. **Comprehend** How were each of these inventions created?

3. **Analyze** Most of the inventions are now used as toys. What does this **imply** about the people who invented them?

Reading Strategy

Ask Questions

- What questions did you ask yourself as you read?
- Which accidental invention do you use?
- How did asking questions help you understand the selection?

Learning Strategies

Ask Questions

As you read, ask yourself questions. This will help you make sure you understand what you are reading. Try these steps.

- Read part of the selection.
- Look at the key words.
- Look at the pictures for clues.
- Ask yourself questions.
- Use what you already know to help you answer the questions.

Practice

Read this passage. In your notebook, list three questions you could ask to be sure you understand it.

> Silly Putty® was <mark>invented</mark> by accident. It can do a lot more than stretch and bounce. It can also pick up an image from a piece of paper. Press Silly Putty onto a comic book. See what happens when you peel if off the paper.

1. _____

2. _____

3. _____

Use a T-Chart

Use a T-Chart to help make sure you understand what you are reading.

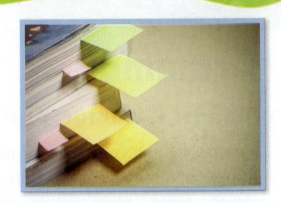

143

Practice

Read this passage from the selection.

> In 1968, scientist Spencer Silver was researching **adhesives** when he **discovered** one that stuck to things, but could then be easily removed. For years he tried to find a use for his invention. At the same time, another scientist named Art Fry sang in a **choir**. He used small scraps of paper to keep track of songs in his songbook. But they always fell out. He needed bookmarks that would stay in place. Silver and Fry put their heads together and created the Post-it® Note.

- Copy the T-Chart in your notebook. Fill in how to find the answer to number 3.
- Add your own question. Tell how you can answer it.

Question	How to Find the Answers
1. What did Spencer Silver accidentally invent?	I could reread the passage.
2. What does **discovered** mean?	I could look back at the keywords page.
3. How did Art Fry use the Post-it notes?	

Extension

You have learned about some of the accidental inventions that people throughout history have made. Which invention in the selection do you like the best? Draw a picture of it. Present your drawing to the class.

Apply

Summarize the selection for a partner.
Use some of the key words as you speak.

Grammar

Nouns: Common and Proper

A **proper noun** names a specific person, place, or thing.
Proper nouns begin with a capital letter. A **common noun**
names a person, place, or thing, but it is not specific.
Common nouns do not begin with a capital letter.
Review the chart:

Catagory	Common Nouns	Proper Nouns
People	a boy a woman	Pablo Mary Smith
Places and Locations	a continent a tourist attraction	South America the Great Wall of China
Titles	my doctor my teacher	Dr. Morgan Mrs. Garcia
Relationships	my aunt my uncle	Aunt Rocio Uncle José
Time Periods	last year the nineties	the Middle Ages the Iron Age
Ethnic or National Groups	the tribe the people	Apaches Irish
Bodies of Water	ocean river	Pacific Ocean Mekong River
Toys	a game an invention	Monopoly Play-Doh
Holidays	a special day a holiday	New Year's Day Labor Day

Circle the proper noun in each sentence. Write the correct form.

1. Do you want to play checkers or (monopoly)? _____Monopoly_____

2. Does paco like to look at fireworks? _____

3. We visited the great barrier reef last year. _____

4. An asian inventor developed that toy. _____

5. I learned about helping others from ms. baker. _____

6. Did you know that ben franklin discovered electricity? _____

Practice B

Read the questions in Apply silently. Write your responses to the questions in your notebook.

Apply

Ask and answer the questions with a partner.

Example: A: Who is our teacher?

B: Our teacher is Mrs. McCoy.

- What are the names of two classmates?
- What is your mother's name?
- What street do you live on?
- Where were you born?
- What country would you like to visit?
- What do you call your aunt or uncle?

Grammar Check ✔

Name a **common noun** and a **proper noun**. Use each one in a sentence.

144

Writing

Explain a Process

When you write, your ideas must be well organized. This is especially important when you are explaining a process.

Writing Prompt

Write a paragraph explaining a process. Include details about steps and materials. Be sure to use common and proper nouns correctly.

① **Prewrite**
GO 4

Invent a new drink. Think about the steps you will need to make your drink. List your ideas in a Sequence Chart.

A student named Adam listed his ideas like this:

② **Draft**

Use your Sequence Chart to help you write a first draft.

- Keep in mind your purpose—to explain a process.
- Include all the steps and materials.

How to Make Juice

First, choose your main ingredient, for example, oranges or lemons.

↓

Second, choose other ingredients you want to add, for example, milk, ice cream, coconut water, etc.

↓

Third, choose a sweetener, for example, honey, sugar, or sugarcane juice.

↓

Fourth, squeeze the juice from the fruit and mix all the ingredients.

↓

Fifth, think of a name for your invention!

↓

Finally, pour the juice into a glass and enjoy!

③ Revise

Read your draft. Look for places where the writing needs improvement. Use the Writing Checklist to help you find problems. Then revise your draft.

④ Edit

Check your work for errors. Use the Peer Review Checklist on page 402.

⑤ Publish

Make a clean copy of your final draft. Share it with the class. Save your work. You will need it for the Writing Workshop.

> **Writing Checklist**
>
> ✔ **Organization**
> I included all the steps in the correct sequence.
> I mentioned what materials I used.
>
> ✔ **Conventions**
> I used common and proper nouns correctly.
> I used sequence words correctly.

Here is Adam's explanation of how to make his favorite drink:

Adam Jensen

I'm learning about inventions in my class. I decided to invent my own drink. I gathered the ingredients I wanted to put in my drink. They included three kinds of fruit. I chose oranges, bananas, and strawberries. I also wanted to add a sweetener. I chose honey. Here's how I made my drink:

First, I squeezed juice from the oranges and poured it into a blender. Then I added the banana and strawberries. Next, I added honey and turned on the blender to mix all the ingredients. Finally, I named my drink orbanberry juice, poured it into a glass, and drank it all up!

145–146

Apply and Extend

Link the Readings

Read the words in the top row. Write your responses in the chart.

- For *On Your Bike, Get Set, Donate!*, put an X under the words that remind you of the selection.

- Repeat the same activity for the other readings.

	Informational text	Literature	Solving problems	Creating things
On Your Bike, Get Set, Donate!				
Scientists and Crows				
Accidental Inventions				

Discussion

1. In the selection *On Your Bike, Get Set, Donate!*, how do volunteers help people in need?

2. How do the scientists in the selection *Scientists and Crows* test their **theory** about crows?

3. How do the inventions described in *Accidental Inventions* help us learn more about them?

 What are some great ideas that make our world a better place?

Listening Skills

If you don't understand a word or phrase, you can say, "What does that mean?"

Projects

Your teacher will help you choose one of these projects.

Written ✎	Oral 💬	Visual/Active 👏
Invent It Think of a new invention. Describe what it might look like and what it could do. You may also want to include a labeled diagram.	**Show and Tell** Think about something important that you use every day. How does it help you? Show and tell why it is important to you.	**Logo** You're the founder of the Book Exchange Club for Kids. Create a logo for your book exchange club. The logo should show images that will tell people about your club. Show your logo to the class and explain what the images mean.
Poem A good poem can start with just one idea. Think of a great idea you want to share. Write about it in a poem.	**Group Plan** Work with a group. Talk about ways to help some younger children. Choose one idea. Make a plan. Explain it to the class.	**Mime** Think of some great inventions. Choose one and act out how to use it. Your classmates must guess what it is.

WB
147–148

Listening and Speaking Workshop

Give a Presentation

You are going to write and give a presentation. Then you will listen as your classmates give their presentations.

① Prepare

A. Choose a favorite hobby or interest you have. You will describe your hobby or interest and explain why you like it. Then your classmates will ask questions about your presentation.

B. Think about what you want to tell your classmates. What is the main idea? What are the details? Find photos, posters, or other props to show during your presentation.

> **Useful Language**
>
> 🎧 Listen and repeat.
>
> I'm going to talk about ...
>
> I like/love ... very much.
>
> I love to ... on weekends.
>
> I also like to read about ...
>
> I always ...
>
> I want to ...
>
> Does anyone have any questions?

> I like science and space. And I'm going to talk about exploring the night sky. It's my favorite hobby.
>
> I read about different stars and planets and constellations. Then I try to find them with my telescope. This is my telescope. And this is my "Star List." I always keep a list of what I find. Last year, I found 10 stars, 5 planets, and 12 constellations.

② Practice

Practice your presentation with your props. Practice in front of your family or friends. If possible, record your presentation. Then listen to yourself. How do you sound? Record yourself again and try to improve.

③ Present

As you speak, do the following:

- Speak clearly and loudly.
- Show your props.
- After your presentation, answer your classmates' questions.

As you listen, do the following:

- Look at the speaker's props. They will help you understand what you hear.
- Think of questions to ask the speaker after the presentation.

④ Evaluate

After you speak, answer these questions:

✔ Did you describe your hobby or interest clearly?

✔ Did you explain why you like it?

After you listen, answer these questions:

✔ Was the presentation formal or informal?

✔ Think about the general meaning of the presentation. Can you think of a title for it? Tell your idea to the class.

Speaking Skills

Presentations can use formal or informal language. Choose which to use based on your audience and the purpose of your presentation.

Listening Skills

Listen carefully for the speaker's main points and important details. Retell these ideas in your own words to confirm that you have understood them.

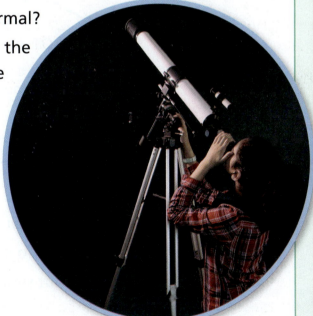

Writing Workshop
Write to Compare and Contrast

Writing Prompt

Write an essay comparing and contrasting two people, things, or places. Describe similarities and differences. Group them in a logical order. Use a Venn Diagram for your comparison. Use transition words, like *although* and *however*.

① Prewrite
GO 2

Review the writing you have done in this unit. Then choose two people, things, or places to compare and contrast. List your points in a Venn Diagram.

A student named Angelina decided to compare and contrast two characters. Angelina listed her ideas like this:

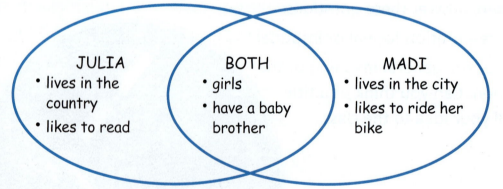

JULIA
• lives in the country
• likes to read

BOTH
• girls
• have a baby brother

MADI
• lives in the city
• likes to ride her bike

② Draft

Use your Venn Diagram to help you write a first draft.

• Keep in mind your purpose—to compare and contrast.

• Include specific details about similarities and differences.

Revise

Read your draft. Look for places where the writing needs improvement. Use the Writing Checklist to help you find problems. Then revise your draft.

Here is how Angelina revised her essay:

Six Traits of Writing Checklist

 Ideas
Did I explain the similarities and differences between the two subjects?

 Organization
Did I organize the essay into paragraphs, grouping similarities and differences in a logical order?

 Voice
Did I use an energetic, lively, and informative voice?

 Word Choice
Did I use transition words like *although* and *however*, to show similarities and differences?

 Sentence Fluency
Did I use a variety of sentence lengths and patterns?

✔ **Conventions**
Did my writing follow the rules of grammar, punctuation, usage, and mechanics?

Angelina Castro

The characters from the story "Country Girl, City Girl" are alike. Although there are some things that are different between them, there ~~is~~ *are* also some important similarities.

Julia ~~growed~~ *grew* up on a farm and she likes to sit inside and read, but Madi would rather be outside riding her bike.

However, in very important ways, Julia and Madi are both alike. Julia has a baby brother named Sam. Madi also has a baby brother. His name is Clay.

Julia and Madi are alike in one very important way. They *both* love their baby brothers!

Revised to correct verb agreement error.

Revised to correct verb tense.

Revised to make meaning clearer.

④ Edit

Check your work for errors. Trade papers with a partner to get feedback. Use the Peer Review Checklist.

⑤ Publish

Make a clean copy of your final draft. Share it with the class.

149–150

Fluency

Listen to the sentences. Pay attention to the groups of words. Read aloud.

1. Many volunteer groups fix up old bicycles to donate to other people.

2. Scientists want to find out if crows use instinct or tools to solve problems.

3. Many everyday inventions were accidental.

Work in pairs. Take turns reading the passage below aloud for one minute. Count the number of words you read.

In 1948, George de Mestral was hiking with his dog. As they walked, he	14
noticed **cockleburs** sticking to his pants and his dog's fur. He wondered	26
how they were able to stick so well. He decided to take a few of the	42
cockleburs to examine under a **microscope**. He saw that the cockleburs	53
had tiny hooks that grabbed hold of the loops in the fabric of his pants.	68
He then figured out a way to copy the hook and loop. His invention	82
became Velcro® Brand Fasteners.	86

With your partner, find the words that slowed you down.

- Practice saying each word and then say the sentence each word is in.

- Then take turns reading the text again. Count the number of words you read.

W B
151

Taking Tests

You will often take tests that help show what you know. Follow these tips to improve your test-taking skills.

> ### Coaching Corner
>
> **Answering Questions That Have Pictures or Graphics**
>
> - Many test questions come with pictures or graphics.
>
> - Before reading the selection, look at the graphic. Make sure you know what it is about.
>
> - Next, read the questions and answer choices.
>
> - Then read any text that comes with it.
>
> - After you read the selection, read the questions. Look at the graphic or picture again.
>
> - Then choose the best answer.
>
> - Check to make sure your answer choices make sense.

Read the selection and information in the chart. Then answer the questions.

My Neighbor's Garden

My neighbor loves to garden. She decided to turn a run-down empty lot on our block into a beautiful garden. In the spring, she asked the kids on the block to help her plant the garden. We planted lots of different vegetables. In the summer, my neighbor asked the kids to help her water and weed the garden. We worked for hours. Soon, the garden was bursting with vegetables! My neighbor asked the kids to help pick the vegetables. She shared them with the neighborhood. Soon there was a block party. All the neighbors brought food they had prepared with vegetables from the garden!

Main Idea: _____		
Detail There are vegetables in the garden.	**Detail** Kids helped the lady plant the garden.	**Detail** The neighbors _____ vegetables from the garden.

1 The main idea is—

A how kids can eat better.

B the lady in the garden.

C how to eat vegetables.

D the neighborhood garden.

2 Who helped the lady in the garden?

F her husband

G kids from the neighborhood

H kids from local schools

J her sister

3 Which word belongs on the blank in the last detail?

A eat

B sleep

C drive

D hate

Tips

✓ Be careful. Make sure you know the difference between a main idea and details.

✓ You can almost always get rid of answers that don't make sense. Which answers don't make sense?

Unit 5

Neighbors in Space

The sun, moon, stars, and planets are Earth's neighbors in space.

Reading 1
Science

Space

Reading 2
Myths

One Moon, Many Myths

Reading 3
Biography

Franklin's Dream

THE BiG QUESTION

What can we learn about Earth and the solar system?

Listening and Speaking

You will talk about stars, planets, and astronauts. In the Listening and Speaking Workshop, you will present a TV newscast.

Writing

You will practice persuasive writing. In the Writing Workshop, you will write a review.

Quick Write

Why does the moon change size and shape? Write what you think.

View and Respond

Talk about the poster for this unit. Then watch and listen to the video and answer the questions at Pearson English Portal.

Words to Know

Listen and repeat. Use these words to talk about space.

 Earth

 moon

 sun

 stars

Practice

Work with a partner. Ask and answer questions.

during the day	at night	both day and night

Example: A: When do you see <u>stars</u>?

B: I see <u>stars</u> at <u>night</u>.

Write

Read the questions. Write your answers in your notebook.

What do you see in the sky at night? What do you see in the sky during the day?

Make Connections

Read the sentences. Write your answers in the spaces provided.

1. I'm made of rock. Sometimes I look round and sometimes I look like only part of a circle. You can see me at night and often during the day. What am I? _____

   a. the sun   **b.** the moon   **c.** the stars

2. I am very hot and very bright. You can hurt your eyes if you look at me. You can see me only during the day. What am I? _____

   a. the sun   **b.** the moon   **c.** the stars

3. You can see us only at night. There are millions of us. We are very bright, like your sun, but we are very far away. What are we? _____

   a. the sun   **b.** the moon   **c.** the stars

What about you?

Talk with a partner. Astronauts train to travel to and work in space. Would you like to be an astronaut? Why or why not?

Kids' Stories from around the World 🎧

England

U.S.A.

Chile

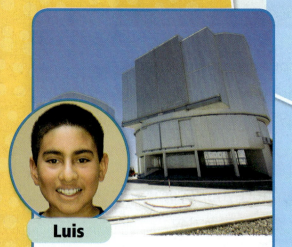

Luis

I live in Chile. One of the biggest telescopes in the world is here. It is called the Very Large Telescope, or VLT. It is four large telescopes that can work together. The VLT is on a high mountain in the desert.

Fiona

When I grow up, I want to be an astronaut. I just came back from Space Camp in Alabama, U.S.A. There, we learned how it feels to travel in space. We trained like real astronauts. We got to eat space food. We even met an astronaut!

Philippines

Rodel

We have star parties here in the Philippines. We go to the best places to see the stars. People bring telescopes. We look at the moon and planets, too. Some people take pictures of the night sky.

Margaret

I live in England, near Stonehenge. Stonehenge is a large circle of very big stones that was made about 5,000 years ago. No one knows how it was built. Some scientists think people used Stonehenge to mark changes in the sun and moon. It may have been a kind of calendar.

What about you?

1. Do you know a lot about space? If yes, how did you learn? If no, do you want to learn more?

2. Do you have a story about Earth's neighbors in space? Share your story.

Key Words

Earth and Beyond tells about the Earth, moon, sun, and stars.

Words in Context

1 The teacher holds a blue **sphere** in one hand. It is a globe. It shows what Earth looks like.

2 Large rocks hit the moon and made **craters**.

3 How many grains of sand are on a beach? **Billions**!

What You Will Learn

Reading
- Vocabulary building: *Context, word study*
- Reading strategy: *Use prior knowledge*
- Text type: *Informational text (science)*

Grammar
Compound sentences (*and* and *but*)

Writing
Write a persuasive paragraph

These words will help you understand the reading.

Key Words

sphere

craters

billions

planets

rotates

continents

4 Earth is one of eight **planets** in our solar system. All eight planets travel around the sun.

5 Earth **rotates**, or turns, on its axis as it travels around the sun.

6 How many **continents** are there?

Practice

Add a page to your vocabulary notebook.

- Divide your page into three columns: the new words, their definitions, and drawings of the words when possible.
- Test yourself by covering one of the columns.

Make Connections

Some people say they feel small when they look at the stars. How do you feel when you look at the night sky? What does it make you think about?

155

These words will help you talk about the reading.

Academic Words

assign
give a duty or task

consist of
be made up of

Academic Words

Words in Context

Teachers often **assign** homework to students.

Stars are giant balls in the sky that **consist of** hot gas.

Practice

Choose an academic word or phrase to complete each sentence.

1. A story _____ three main parts: plot, character, and setting.

2. Our parents _____ each of us chores to do on Saturdays.

Apply

Ask and answer with a partner.

1. What chores at home would you like to **assign** to someone else?

2. A diet is the food you regularly eat. What kinds of foods does your usual diet **consist of**?

W B
156

Word Study

Synonyms and Antonyms

Synonyms are words that mean the same thing.
(earth—world)
Antonyms are words that have opposite meanings.
(big—small)

Practice

Work with a partner. Choose a synonym or an antonym for each underlined word.

> **Synonyms**
> sphere   large   surface

1. Earth is a <u>big</u> ball in space.

2. Like Earth, the moon is a <u>ball</u>.

3. The <u>outside</u> of the moon is dusty.

> **Antonyms**
> cold   bright   night

4. Look up at the <u>day</u> sky.

5. The sun is very <u>dim</u>.

6. The temperature on the moon can be very <u>hot</u>.

Informational Text
Science

More About THE BiG QUESTION

What can we learn about Earth and the solar system?

🎧 **Listen to the Audio.**
Listen for the main points and important details.

Reading Strategy

Use Prior Knowledge

Think about what you already know about a topic. This can prepare you to learn more. Before you read, ask yourself:

- What do I already know?
- What do I want to find out?

Listen as your teacher models the reading strategy.

Earth and Beyond

by Maya Hightower

We live on Earth. Earth is a sphere. It is a large, round ball in space. But Earth is not alone.

Look up at the night sky. What do you want to learn? What are stars made of? Do people live on the moon?

Look up at the sky in the day. What do you want to learn? How big is the sun? Why can't you see stars during the day?

The more you look, the more questions you will have. Let's travel through space to find some answers.

Reading Skill

Before you read, look for difficult words. Look up their meanings. Then read the article.

What do we know about the moon?

The moon is our nearest neighbor in space. It is 239,000 miles (384,833 kilometers) from Earth.

The moon is a sphere, like Earth. The surface of the moon is dusty. It has mountains and plains. Many <mark>craters</mark> cover the moon's **surface**.

Do people live on the moon?

No! The moon does not have air. The **temperature** can change from very hot to very cold. No plants, animals, or people can live on the moon.

Have people ever visited the moon?

Yes! Twelve **astronauts** have walked on the moon. They wore special suits so they could breathe. They brought back moon rocks.

---

surface top or outside

temperature measure of how hot or cold
something is

astronaut someone who travels and
works in space

Before You Go On

Why can't people live on the moon?

What are stars?

Stars look like tiny lights in the sky, but they are giant balls of hot gas.

How many stars are there?

There are <mark>billions</mark> of stars in space, but we can't see all of them. On a clear night, we can see thousands of stars.

Why do stars look so small?

Stars look small because they are so far away.

What is a constellation?

A constellation is a group of stars that looks like a picture. Long ago, people looked up at the night sky. They saw shapes made by the stars. People named these shapes for things they knew, such as animals.

What is the sun?

The sun is a star. Earth and the other planets **orbit** the sun.

Why does the sun look so big and bright?

It looks big and bright because it is closer than any other star. The sun is so bright that we can't see other stars during the day.

The sun is always glowing. So why is the sky dark at night?

Earth rotates every 24 hours. When our side of Earth faces the sun, we have day. When our side faces away from the sun, we have night.

Why is the sun so important?

The sun warms and lights Earth.

Can people visit the sun?

No! The sun is too hot.

---

orbit   travel in a circle in space around a larger object

Before You Go On

How did people assign names to constellations?

What is the solar system?

The solar system is like a large neighborhood. It is made up of the sun and all the things that orbit the sun. Earth and its moon are part of the solar system. So are other planets and their moons. The solar system also has billions of **asteroids** and **meteors**.

What is a planet?

A planet is a large sphere that rotates in space as it orbits the sun. Some planets are made of rock, and others are made of gas. Some have rings around them, and some have many moons.

What are the planets in the solar system?

Mercury, Venus, Earth, Mars, Jupiter, Saturn, Uranus, and Neptune are the planets.

---

asteroids   small, rocky objects that move around the sun

meteors   pieces of rock or metal that float in space

What is special about the planet Earth?

Earth has water and air. It is the only planet where people, animals, and plants can live.

What does Earth look like from space?

Earth looks like a beautiful ball with many colors. From space, the oceans look blue and the ==continents== look brown and green.

158–160

Reading Strategy

Use Prior Knowledge

- What did you already know before you read?
- What did you want to find out?
- How did thinking about these questions help you understand the selection?

Think It Over

1. **Recall** What does the solar system **consist** of?
2. **Comprehend** What causes day and night?
3. **Analyze** Many objects in space share the same shape. What is it?

Learning Strategies

The 5W Questions

Before you read, think about your purpose for reading. Often we read because we want to learn something. You can help yourself learn more effectively by asking yourself questions that begin with these words:

Who? What? Where? When? Why?

These questions are sometimes called the 5Ws. They focus on people, events, time, places, and reasons.

Practice

With a partner, read *Earth and Beyond* again. Look for answers to the following questions.

1. Who has visited the moon?
2. What does the surface of the moon look like?
3. Where are the moon's craters located?
4. When is it daytime? When is it nighttime?
5. Why can't we see stars during the day?

Use a K-W-L Chart

What did you already know about space? What did you want to learn? A K-W-L Chart can help you see what you have learned.

Practice
GO 5

Complete all three columns. Share your work with a partner.

What I **K**now	What I **W**ant to Know	What I **L**earned
I know the moon is in the night sky.	Do people live on the moon?	1. No. There is no air on the moon. 2. No plants, animals, or people can live there.

161

Apply

Summarize the selection. Use some of the key words as you speak.

Extension

Work in small groups. Choose a planet. Do research independently about the planet your group has chosen. Share your information with your group. Then create a poster together. Share it with the class.

Grammar

Compound Sentences

A **simple sentence** has one independent clause and expresses one idea or thought. These are examples of simple sentences.

> Oceans look blue.
> Both the sun and the moon help Earth.
> Earth needs both the sun and the moon.

To make a compound sentence, join two simple sentences that are related. Use a connecting word such as **and** or **but**. Put a comma (,) before the connecting word.

> Earth's oceans look blue. (+) The <mark>continents</mark> look brown.
> Earth's oceans look blue, **and** the continents look brown.

Use **and** to simply **add** another complete thought. Use **but** to show a **contrast** or **difference** between two complete thoughts.

Simple Sentence	(+)	**Simple Sentence**
There are <mark>billions</mark> of stars in space.		We can't see all of them.

Compound Sentence
There are billions of stars in space, **but** we can't see all of them.

Practice A

Join each pair of sentences to make a compound sentence. Use *and* or *but*. Write the compound sentences in your notebook.

1. It was cloudy. I saw some stars.

   It was cloudy, but I saw some stars.

2. Stars look so tiny in the sky. They are actually really big!

3. The sun warms Earth. It also gives us light.

4. Some planets have rings around them. Others do not.

5. Constellations are groups of stars. They form different shapes.

Practice B

**Answer the questions in Apply. Use compound sentences.
Write your answers in your notebook.**

Apply

**Work with a partner. Ask and answer the questions.
Use the answers you wrote in Practice B.**

Example: A: How did you get to school today, and how will
   you get home?

   B: I rode the bus to school, and I'll ride the bus
   home, too.

- Where did you eat breakfast yesterday, and where did you eat lunch?
- What time do you wake up on Mondays, and what time do you wake up on Saturdays?
- What subject do you like, and what subject do you *really* like?

> **Grammar Check** ✔
>
> Write a **compound sentence** using *and* or *but*.

162

Writing

Write a Persuasive Paragraph

In a persuasive paragraph, your goal is to persuade the reader to agree with you.

Writing Prompt

Write a persuasive paragraph about whether you think learning about space is important. Be sure to use compound sentences, and to use the connecting words *and* and *but* correctly.

① **Prewrite**

Decide whether you think learning about space is important. List the ideas that support your belief in a chart.

A student named Kim listed her ideas like this:

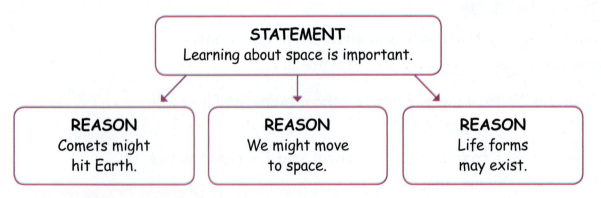

② **Draft**

Use your chart to help you write a first draft.
- Keep in mind your purpose—to persuade the reader.
- Include reasons for your belief.

③ Revise

Reread your draft. Look for places where it needs improvement. Use the Writing Checklist to help you find problems. Then revise your draft.

④ Edit

Check your work for errors. Use the Peer Review Checklist on page 402.

⑤ Publish

Make a clean copy of your final draft. Share it with the class. Save your work for the Writing Workshop.

Here is Kim's persuasive paragraph:

Kim Yang

Learning about space is important. There are many reasons why. First, scientists need to know if a comet is going to hit the Earth and when. Second, the number of people on the Earth is growing too large. We may have to move to another planet someday. Third, it is important to find out if life forms exist on other planets. Space exploration is expensive, but it will benefit everyone.

163–164

What You Will Learn

Reading
- Vocabulary building: *Context, word study*
- Reading strategy: *Compare and contrast*
- Text type: *Literature (myths)*

Grammar
Future: *be going to*

Writing
Write a prediction

These words will help you understand the reading.

Key Words

bark

rainbow

canoe

handprints

Key Words

In *One Moon, Many Myths,* you will read different myths about the moon.

Words in Context

1 The **bark** of a tree is its outer covering. Different trees have different kinds of bark.

2 You can see a **rainbow** when the sun shines through drops of water. This can happen in the sky. It can also happen close to you.

3 This family paddles a **canoe**. They wear life jackets to be safe.

4 Native Americans made these **handprints** on a cave wall long ago.

Practice

Draw pictures of the key words. Label each picture with a sentence that contains the key word.

Make Connections

What do you look at in nature? Do you look at the **bark** on trees? Have you ever seen a **rainbow**? Describe what you like to look at when you are outside.

These words will help you talk about the reading.

Academic Words

phenomenon
something we can observe, or see

traditional
following ideas or methods that have existed for a long time

Academic Words

Words in Context

Sometimes a **phenomenon** is uncommon, such as a double rainbow.

My grandfather makes a **traditional** dessert that his mother made when he was little.

Practice

Choose an academic word to complete each sentence. Write your answers in the blanks.

1. The northern lights are a natural
   _____. They sometimes appear in the night sky.

2. My aunt wears a hanbok, the _____ Korean dress, to our family celebrations.

Apply

Ask and answer with a partner.

1. Which natural **phenomenon** is the most frightening? A tornado, a hurricane, or an earthquake? Why do you think so?

2. What **traditional** events does your town have in the summer or during the holidays? Describe them.

Word Study

Multiple-Meaning Words

Some words have more than one meaning, such as the word *bark*.

1. The **bark** on this tree is brown.

2. Look at the dog **bark**!

> **bark¹** outer covering of a tree
> **bark²** make a short, loud sound

Practice

**Work with a partner. Read each sentence.
Choose the best meaning for the underlined word.**

1. Last night I <u>saw</u> a full moon.

> **saw¹** looked at
> **saw²** a tool with a sharp blade

2. It's not raining hard. It's only raining a little <u>bit</u>.

> **bit¹** took a bite of
> **bit²** small amount

Literature
Myths

More About **THE BIG QUESTION**

Why did people long ago make up stories to explain things in space?

🎧 **Listen to the Audio.**
Listen for the main points and important details.

Reading Strategy

Compare and Contrast

Comparing and contrasting helps you to understand ideas in a text.

• To compare, look for ways the myths are the same.

• To contrast, look for ways the myths are different.

Listen as your teacher models the reading strategy.

One Moon, Many Myths

by Ona Mecklei
illustrated by Joel Nakamura

Long ago, people looked up at the sky and asked questions. They wanted to know where clouds came from, and how the sun got in the sky. They wondered about the moon. Why did it disappear? How did it reappear? People made up stories to explain these natural events. The stories are called myths.

When the Hawaiian people saw white, puffy clouds filling the sky, they wondered, "How did the clouds get there?" A myth gave them an explanation.

Hina and the Moon

Long ago, people made cloth from bark. They beat the bark, and it became soft cloth.

Hina lived on Earth long ago. One night, she saw a full moon. A rainbow stretched from the moon to Earth.

"I will climb to the moon," she said. And she did.

Hina began to beat bark. The cloth was white. She threw her cloth over Earth. The cloth became a cloud.

Hina is still on the moon to this day, making clouds.

Before You Go On

What traditional task does Hina perform while she is on the moon?

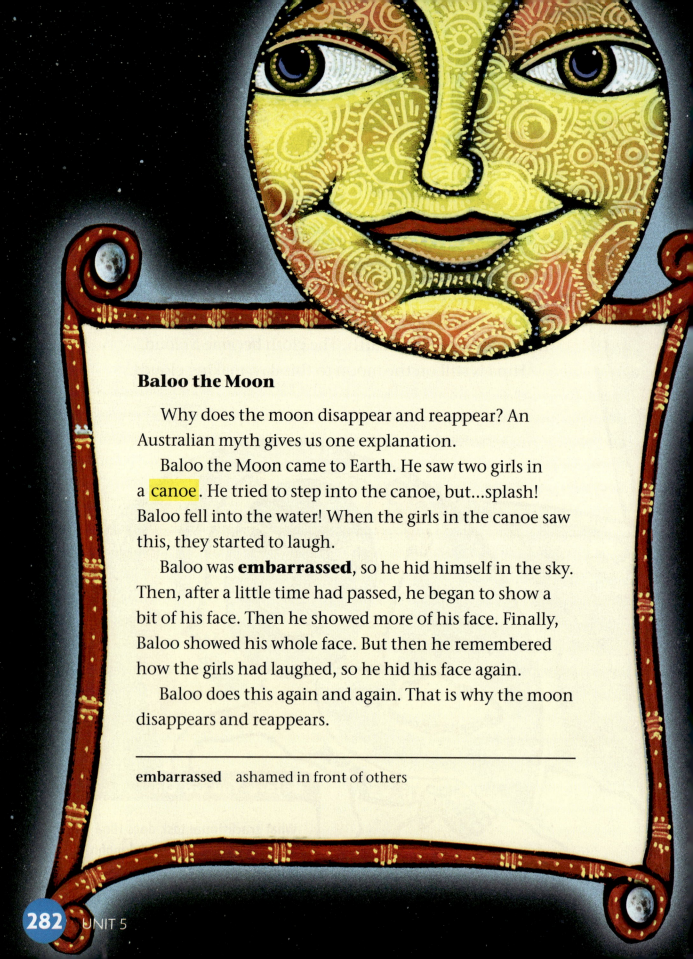

Baloo the Moon

Why does the moon disappear and reappear? An Australian myth gives us one explanation.

Baloo the Moon came to Earth. He saw two girls in a canoe. He tried to step into the canoe, but...splash! Baloo fell into the water! When the girls in the canoe saw this, they started to laugh.

Baloo was **embarrassed**, so he hid himself in the sky. Then, after a little time had passed, he began to show a bit of his face. Then he showed more of his face. Finally, Baloo showed his whole face. But then he remembered how the girls had laughed, so he hid his face again.

Baloo does this again and again. That is why the moon disappears and reappears.

---

embarrassed   ashamed in front of others

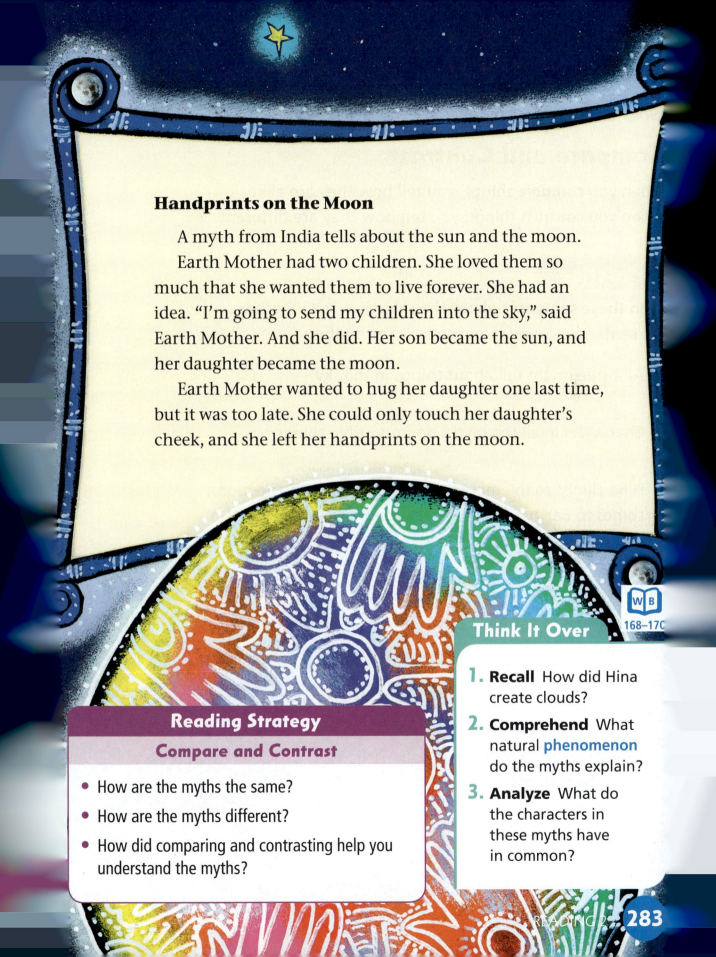

Handprints on the Moon

A myth from India tells about the sun and the moon.

Earth Mother had two children. She loved them so much that she wanted them to live forever. She had an idea. "I'm going to send my children into the sky," said Earth Mother. And she did. Her son became the sun, and her daughter became the moon.

Earth Mother wanted to hug her daughter one last time, but it was too late. She could only touch her daughter's cheek, and she left her handprints on the moon.

WB 168–170

Think It Over

1. **Recall** How did Hina create clouds?

2. **Comprehend** What natural **phenomenon** do the myths explain?

3. **Analyze** What do the characters in these myths have in common?

Reading Strategy

Compare and Contrast

- How are the myths the same?
- How are the myths different?
- How did comparing and contrasting help you understand the myths?

Learning Strategies

Compare and Contrast

When you **compare** things, you tell how they are alike.
When you **contrast** things, you tell how they are different.

Practice

Read these sentences about the selection. Tell whether the sentences compare or contrast the myths.

1. All three myths tell about things in the sky.

2. Characters in all the myths do impossible things.

3. Hina climbs to the moon on a rainbow. Baloo the moon comes to Earth. Earth Mother's children become the sun and moon.

4. All three myths explain something in nature.

5. Hina makes the clouds. Baloo makes the moon appear and disappear. Earth Mother made handprints on the moon.

Use a Venn Diagram

A Venn Diagram can help you compare and contrast. The outside of the circles tells what is different. The part where the circles link tells what is alike.

Practice

GO 2

Copy and complete the diagram.

1. Compare and contrast the two myths.
2. Make another Venn Diagram. Compare and contrast the Indian myth with the Baloo myth or the Hina myth.

BALOO MYTH   HINA MYTH

1. Tells why the moon disappears and appears again
2. Comes from Australia
3. _____

1. Explains something in nature
2. _____

1. Tells where clouds come from
2. Comes from Hawaii
3. _____

W B
171

Apply

Choose one of the myths you read. Retell it to a partner.

Extension

Create a myth that tells why there are so many stars in the sky. Share your myth with the class.

Grammar

Future: *be going to*

To talk about the future, you can use *be going to* or *will*.

Past   **Now**   **Future**

> "I**'m going to** send my children into the sky," said Earth Mother.
> "I **will** climb to the moon," Hina said.

The *be going to* form is used more frequently than *will*. Use **be going to** + verb to talk about prior plans or decisions made before the moment of speaking.

> I**'m going to watch** a movie on Saturday. (prior plan)

Use **be going to** + verb to predict when there are signs that something is going to happen.

> The sky is very dark. It**'s going to rain**. (prediction)

To make a negative sentence, use a form of **be** + **not** + g**o**ing **to** + the base form of a verb.

> She's sick. She**'s not going to go** to school tomorrow.

Practice A

Complete the sentences with the correct form of
be going to **+ the verb in parentheses.**

1. We <u>are going to watch</u> a video about Earth today. **(watch)**

2. My teacher _____ us a test this afternoon. **(give)**

3. I _____ tonight. **(study)**

4. She didn't study. She _____ an A on the test. **(not get)**

5. They're tired. They _____ after school. **(not practice)**

Practice B

Answer these questions in your notebook.

1. What are you going to do tonight?

2. What are you going to be when you grow up?

Apply

Work with a partner. Ask and answer the questions. Use ***be going to.***

Example: A: Are you going to walk home?

B: Yes, I'm going to walk home.

- Is your family going to watch television tonight?
- Are you going to study later?
- Are you going to call anyone?
- Are you going to be home this weekend?

Grammar Check ✔

Write a sentence using the **future with *be going to*.**

Writing

Write a Prediction

A prediction is a statement about what you think is going to happen. To make a prediction persuasive, support it with reasons.

Writing Prompt

Write a prediction about where you think scientists are going to travel in space next. Give reasons to support your prediction. Be sure to use *be going to* correctly.

① Prewrite

Decide where you think scientists are going to travel next in space. List reasons to support your prediction in a graphic organizer.

A student named Kaisha listed her ideas like this:

PREDICTION
I predict that scientists are going to explore the moon again.

REASON
We learned that there is water on the moon.

REASON
We can use the moon as a station.

② Draft

Use your graphic organizer to help you write a first draft.

- Keep in mind your purpose—to make a prediction.
- Include reasons that support your prediction.

Revise

Reread your draft. Look for places where it needs improvement. Use the Writing Checklist to help you find problems. Then revise your draft.

Edit

Check your work for errors. Do Peer Review (use the Checklist on page 402).

⑤ Publish

Make a clean copy of your final draft. Share it with the class. Save your work. You will need it for the Writing Workshop.

Here is Kaisha's paragraph:

Kaisha Okar

    I predict that scientists are going to explore the Moon again. There are several things that make the Moon important for scientists. Scientists learned recently that there is water on the Moon. There could be enough water to fill a reservoir in Europe. Also, scientists can use the Moon as a station on the way to other planets. This is why I think scientists are going to explore and study the moon again.

173–174

Key Words

Franklin's Dream tells about a boy who grew up to become an astronaut.

Words in Context

1 Astronauts ride a <mark>space shuttle</mark> to go into space and come back to Earth. A trip in space is called a space <mark>flight</mark>.

2 The space shuttle may take a <mark>satellite</mark> into space. A satellite orbits Earth. Satellites help telephones and televisions work.

What You Will Learn

Reading
- Vocabulary building: *Context, phonics*
- Reading strategy: *Summarize*
- Text type: *Informational text (biography)*

Grammar
Complex sentences: *because* and *so*

Writing
Write a persuasive letter

These words will help you understand the reading.

Key Words

space shuttle

flight

satellite

observe

spacewalks

3 Scientists <mark>observe</mark> the stars through a telescope.

4 Astronauts take <mark>spacewalks</mark> to go outside the space shuttle.

Practice

Make flashcards to help you memorize the words.
- Write a key word on the front.
- On the back, write the meaning.

Make Connections

Would you like to be an astronaut?
Why or why not?

175

These words will help you talk about the reading.

Academic Words

emigrate
to leave one's country to settle in another

significant
important

Academic Words

Words in Context

Some people **emigrate** to another country to find a better way of life.

The invention of the cell phone has had a **significant** effect on how we communicate with each other.

Practice

Choose an academic word to complete each sentence. Write your answer in the blank.

1. There is a _____ difference between my old school, which was small, and my new school, which is large.

2. My grandparents _____ to the United States when my mother was a baby.

Apply

Ask and answer with a partner.

1. If you could choose another country to live in, which country would you **emigrate** to? Why?

2. What **significant** events have happened in your school this year?

Phonics

R-Controlled Vowels: *ar, or, ore*

The letter *r* changes vowel sounds. Listen. Then read each word aloud.

am	t**o**n	t**oe**
arm	t**or**n	t**ore**

Rule

The letters *ar* usually have the vowel sound heard in **art**.
The letters *or* and *ore* usually have the vowel sound heard in **born** and **more**.

Practice

Read the sentences with a partner. Take turns.

- Read the sentences aloud. Listen for words that have r-controlled vowels.
- List the words with *ar*.
- List the words with *or* and *ore*.

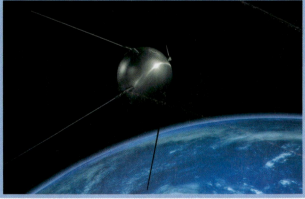

1. His story starts in Costa Rica.

2. That is where he was born.

3. He was a smart child.

4. He enjoyed sports.

5. He wanted to explore space.

Informational Text
Biography

More About THE BiG QUESTION

How can someone become an astronaut?

🎧 **Listen to the Audio.**
Listen for the main points and important details.

Reading Strategy
Summarize

Summarizing a selection helps you check that you understood what you read.

- Think about what is important in the selection.
- Identify the main idea.
- Identify the important details.

Listen as your teacher models the reading strategy.

Franklin's Dream

by Mirna Cepeda

It is 1986. The space shuttle *Columbia* lifts off. Franklin Chang-Diaz is on the shuttle. This is his first space flight. His dream has come true.

Franklin was born in San José, Costa Rica. When he was a boy, he heard about *Sputnik*. *Sputnik* was the first satellite to orbit Earth.

Franklin climbed a mango tree. He watched the sky for hours.

"I was seven years old," he said, "when I decided to become an astronaut."

Franklin never let go of his dream.

Before You Go On

What **significant** event caused Franklin to want to become an astronaut?

Franklin was a good student in school. But that was not all. He was a **curious** child. He liked to observe the things around him. He tried to learn more about them. Sports and music were his hobbies. Science and reading were the **subjects** he liked best. He planned to study science.

---

curious   wanting to know or learn things
subjects   main things you study in school

Reading Skill

If you don't understand something, ask your classmates or your teacher, "What does this mean?" If you think you understand but you want to make sure, ask, "Does this mean…?"

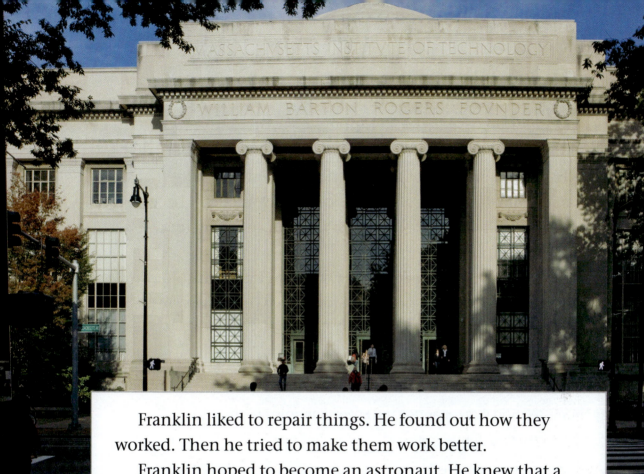

Franklin liked to repair things. He found out how they worked. Then he tried to make them work better.

Franklin hoped to become an astronaut. He knew that a good education would help him. He also knew that he needed to learn English. So he moved to the United States. His parents helped him.

Franklin kept working hard. He learned English, and he studied science. His teachers helped him. He went to **college**. Franklin became a **scientist**.

---

college   school after high school

scientist   someone who works in science

Before You Go On

Why did Franklin and his family **immigrate** to the United States?

In 1980, Franklin was chosen to become an astronaut. He started to train in classrooms and in labs. After six years of training, he was ready. It was 1986, the year of *Columbia's* flight.

Franklin flew on a total of seven space flights—more flights than anyone had ever gone on before. He would later become a director at Johnson Space Center in Houston. He **retired** from **NASA** in 2005.

These days, Franklin is the **CEO** of a **rocket** technology company, and a professor of physics at Rice University and the University of Houston.

---

retired   stopped working

NASA   National Aeronautics and Space Administration

CEO   Chief Executive Officer

rocket   a space vehicle

Flying in space is exciting. But for Franklin, the sight of Earth from outer space is the best part. He says that it is very beautiful. He says that we must take care of Earth.

"Earth is **humanity's** spaceship and the only one we have," says Franklin. "We must protect it."

178–180

---

humanity's belonging to all people

Think It Over

1. **Recall** Where was Franklin born?

2. **Comprehend** Describe Franklin. What was he like as a boy? Give details.

3. **Analyze** How does his experience as an astronaut help him on his current jobs?

Reading Strategy

Summarize

- What was the main idea of the selection?
- What were the important details?

A Closer Look at...

Space Exploration

▲ Blast off!
A space shuttle begins its flight into space.

▲ Docking
Astronauts ride the space shuttle to get to the space station. The space shuttle docks, or links, to the space station.

▲ Spacewalk
An astronaut goes on a spacewalk to work outside the space shuttle.

▲ Space station
This is the International Space Station. People from many countries work here.

▲ Robot on Mars

People have not walked on Mars—yet! But scientists sent this robot there. The robot helped scientists study rocks.

▲ Red planet

A robot took this picture of the surface of Mars. Mars is often called the red planet. Can you tell why?

◀ Moon walk

Buzz Aldrin was an astronaut on the first trip to the moon in 1969.

Activity to Do

These two pages use words and pictures to tell about space exploration.

- Choose another type of exploration

- Find pictures to show that exploration.

- Post your pictures and captions in your classroom.

Learning Strategies

Summarize

To **summarize**, tell only the main idea and the most important details.

Practice

Read these details from the selection. Choose three important details.

1. Franklin was born in Costa Rica.
2. Franklin climbed a mango tree.
3. Franklin moved to the United States and learned English.
4. Franklin's hobbies were sports and music.
5. Franklin worked hard in school. He became a scientist.
6. Flying in space is exciting.
7. Franklin flew on more space flights than anyone had flown before.

Use a Main Idea and Details Chart

A Main Idea and Details Chart can help you summarize what you read.

Practice
GO 1

> ### MAIN IDEA
> Franklin's dream was to become an astronaut.
> He achieved his goal.

DETAIL:
Franklin was born in Costa Rica.

DETAIL:

DETAIL:

Choose two details that support the main idea. Add them to the chart.

1. Franklin climbed a mango tree.
2. Franklin worked hard in school. He became a scientist.
3. Franklin flew on more space flights than anyone had flown before.
4. Flying in space is exciting.

181

Apply

Reread the selection and take notes. Then close your book and retell the selection to a partner.

> ### Extension
> Franklin Chang-Diaz had a dream. Think of a time when you had a special dream. Tell a partner what you did to make your dream come true.

Grammar

Complex Sentences: *because* and *so*

A **clause** is a group of words containing a subject and a verb. These are examples of clauses:

Stars look small. (independent clause)

Because they are so far away (dependent clause).

You can use *because* and *so* to connect clauses. Clauses connected by **because** and **so** are called complex sentences.

> Use *because* to give a reason:
> Stars look small because they are so far away.

> Use *so* to give a result:
> Franklin studied hard so he could become an astronaut.

If the clause with *because* begins the sentence, you should use a comma between the clauses.

> Franklin liked to observe things *because* he was curious.
> Because he was curious, Franklin liked to observe things.

Practice A

Join each pair of sentences to make a complex sentence. Use _because_ or _so_. Write the sentences in your notebook.

1. I look through a telescope. I can see the stars.
   I look through a telescope, so I can see the stars.

2. Many students work hard. They have a goal.

3. People want a better life. They work hard.

4. I try to repair things. I can learn how they work.

5. Astronauts ride the <mark>space shuttle</mark>. They want to explore space.

6. Scientists study space. They want to learn more about it.

Practice B

Complete these sentences with _so_ or _because_.

1. I'm learning English _____.

2. I like learning English _____.

Apply

Work with a partner. Ask and answer the questions. Use a complex sentence in your answer.

Example: A: What sports do you like, and why?

   B: I like soccer because I like to run.

- Are you interested in space? Why or why not?
- Why are students late for school?
- Why do we sometimes work with a partner?
- Why do many people eat a healthy breakfast?

Grammar Check ✔

Write one **complex sentence** using **because** or **so**.

Writing

Write a Persuasive Letter

A persuasive letter is a letter asking someone to help you.

Writing Prompt

Write a business letter to the officials of a space camp to persuade them to accept you as a camper. Give reasons to support your request. Be sure to use compound and complex sentences and the correct connecting words.

① Prewrite

GO 12

Decide why you would benefit from Space Camp. List reasons to support your argument in a Three-Column Chart.

A student named Azra listed her ideas like this:

WHY I SHOULD ATTEND SPACE CAMP		
REASON 1	**REASON 2**	**REASON 3**
I'm in good physical condition.	I might want to be an astronaut when I grow up.	I'm very good at math and science.

② Draft

Use your Three-Column Chart to help you write a first draft.

- Keep in mind your purpose—to persuade the officials to accept you to their <mark>space camp</mark>.
- Include reasons that explain your statement.

③ Revise

Read your draft. Look for places where it needs improvement. Use the Writing Checklist. Then revise your draft.

④ Edit

Check your work for errors. Use the Peer Review Checklist on page 402.

⑤ Publish

Make a clean copy of your final draft. Share it with the class.

Writing Checklist

✔ **Ideas**
I stated my request clearly.

✔ **Organization**
I presented my reasons in a logical order.

✔ **Conventions**
I used compound and complex sentences and the correct connecting words.

Here is Azra's letter:

Ulus Mah

253 Sok.

Beyaz Apt No. 3 Kat 5 D 3

Muğla, Turkiye

Space Camp Turkey

35410 Gaziemir

Izmir, Turkey

To whom it may concern:

Please consider me as a candidate for Space Camp Turkey. I believe I would be a good space camper. First, I exercise regularly, which I know is important for training for space travel. Second, I might want to be an astronaut, and space camp would help me learn more about this important job. Finally, I'm very good at math and science.

Sincerely,

Azra

183–184

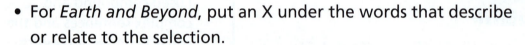

Put It All Together

Apply and Extend

Link the Readings

Read the words in the top row. Write your responses in the blanks.

- For *Earth and Beyond*, put an X under the words that describe or relate to the selection.

- Repeat the same activity for the other readings.

	Informational text	Literature	The moon	Science
Earth and Beyond				
One Moon, Many Myths				
Franklin's Dream				

Discussion

1. What interests and significant events in Franklin's life prepared him to become an astronaut?

2. What objects in space do the three myths talk about?

3. How is *Earth and Beyond* similar to *One Moon, Many Myths?*

What can we know about our neighbors in space?

Listening Skills

When a classmate is making a presentation, don't interrupt. Wait until after the presentation to ask your question.

Projects

Your teacher will help you choose one of these projects.

Written	Oral	Visual/Active
Space Story	**Space Facts**	**Moon Map**
Write a story about an imaginary trip to a planet or a trip to a planet by an astronaut that you know about.	List three facts about any of these: one of the planets, the sun, or the moon. Read your facts aloud. Have a partner guess what part of the solar system it is.	Find a map of the moon on the internet. Make a model of the moon. Make labels to show the craters and seas on the moon.
Planet Song	**Biography Lesson**	**Space Mobile**
Write a song about the planets. Name all the planets. The song should help you learn the order of the planets from the sun.	Pick an astronaut besides Franklin Chang-Diaz. Find out about that astronaut's trip into space. Tell what he or she has done in space.	Make a mobile of our solar system. On the back of each picture, write a fact about it. Hang the mobile in your classroom.

WB 185–186

Listening and Speaking Workshop

Present a TV Newscast

You are going to write and present a TV newscast. Then you will listen as your classmates present their newscasts.

① Prepare

A. Find a partner. Decide on a story about space or space exploration. You will present this story.

B. Each of you will describe a part of the story. Find props or other visuals to use during your newscast.

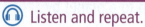

Useful Language

Listen and repeat.

Hi/Hello. Welcome to . . .

We have a/an (great/fun/ interesting) show for you today!

Thanks for watching!

News Anchor 1:	I'm Sam Yee. Here's an interesting story. NASA's dog, Jupiter, landed on Mars this morning.
News Anchor 2:	I'm Tonya Vasquez. And that is interesting, Sam. But here's something truly amazing. At the exact time Jupiter landed on Mars, a dog on Earth named Tiny ran into its front yard and started to jump into the air and bark.
News Anchor 1:	Does anyone know why Tiny did this?

② Practice

Practice your TV newscast in front of your family or friends. As you work together, listen to each other's ideas and work cooperatively.

③ Present

As you speak, do the following:

- Face your audience.
- Speak clearly and loudly.
- Show your props or other visuals.

As you listen, do the following:

- Take notes about *Who*? *What*? *When*? *Where*? and *How*?
- Listen carefully for ideas and information that is not stated directly.
- Pay close attention. Your teacher will ask you questions after the newscast.

④ Evaluate

After you speak, answer these questions:

- ✔ Did your group give details and other important information about the news story?
- ✔ Did your group use formal language?

After you listen, answer these questions:

- ✔ Did the newscasters speak clearly and directly to the audience?
- ✔ Did the newscasters use formal language?

Speaking Skills

Formal language is used during serious situations and when you don't know the people very well. Newscasters usually use formal language.

Listening Skills

Listen carefully for the main points and important details. Retell these ideas in your own words to confirm that you have understood them.

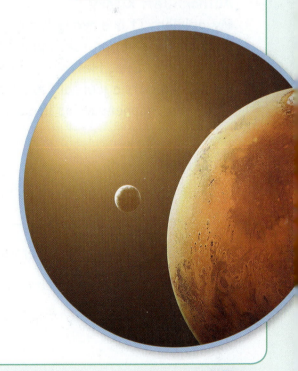

Writing Workshop
Write a Book or Movie Review

Writing Prompt
Write a movie or book review. Include details about the characters, plot, and setting. List this information in a graphic organizer.

① Prewrite

Review the writing you have done in this unit. Now choose a movie or book to review. What is your opinion of it? How can you persuade the reader of your review to agree with you? List your points in a graphic organizer.

A student named Kevin listed his ideas like this:

Title: Diary of a Wimpy Kid
Author: Jeff Kinney
My opinion: It is a really funny book!
Setting: The action takes place at Greg's home and school.
Characters: Greg Heffley, a middle schooler
Plot: Greg gets a journal from his mom, and he writes all about what happens in his life as a kid in middle school.

② Draft

Use your graphic organizer to help you write a first draft.

- Keep in mind your purpose—to write a book review.

- Include details that will persuade the reader to agree with your opinion.

③ Revise

Read your draft. Look for places where the writing needs improvement. Use the Writing Checklist to help you find problems. Then revise your draft.

Here is how Kevin revised his essay:

Six Traits of Writing Checklist

✔ **Ideas**
Did I give reasons to support my opinion?

✔ **Organization**
Did I organize my supporting reasons into paragraphs?

✔ **Voice**
Did I use an informative and persuasive voice?

✔ **Word Choice**
Did I use a variety of adjectives?

✔ **Sentence Fluency**
Did I use a variety of sentence lengths and patterns?

✔ **Conventions**
Did my writing follow the rules of grammar, punctuation, usage, and mechanics?

Kevin Zheng

<u>Diary of a Wimpy Kid</u> by Jeff Kinney is a hilari^ous book!

As the story starts, Greg is just beginning middle school, where he feel^s he doesn't fit in. The school is a good setting for the book. Greg's mother gave him a journal (not a diary!) so he uses it to write about all his troubles.

The story's plot is filled with many funny events. On the first day of school, Greg has to sit with a kid who doesn't fit in, Fregley. Greg also has a best friend named Rowley Jefferson. Together they try to fit in at their middle school. Together Greg and Rowley face many things **such as trying out for wrestling and facing bullies.**

Read <u>Diary of a Wimpy Kid</u> soon. You will be laughing from cover to cover!

Revised
to correct spelling error

Revised
to correct verb agreement error

Revised
to make meaning clearer

Peer Review Checklist

✔ The introduction states the author's opinion.

✔ The ideas and opinions expressed are clear.

✔ The supporting reasons are convincing.

④ Edit

Check your work for errors. Trade papers with a partner to get feedback. Use the Peer Review Checklist on page 404. Edit your final draft in response to feedback from your partner and your teacher.

⑤ Publish

Make a clean copy of your final draft. Share it with the class.

187–188

Spelling Tip

Pay attention to words ending in -se and -ce. American English and British English have different rules about these spellings, so it is common for writers to get them mixed up. You have to memorize how these words are spelled.

Fluency

Listen to the sentences. Pay attention to the groups of words. Read aloud.

1. Some of our neighbors in space are the moon, the sun, stars, and planets.

2. Many different stories explain the behavior of objects in the sky.

3. Franklin Chang-Diaz's dream to become a NASA astronaut came true.

Work in pairs. Take turns reading the text below aloud for one minute. Count the number of words you read.

Franklin's Dream tells the story of a little boy who wanted	11
to fly into space. He moved with his parents from his home in	24
Costa Rica to the United States. He studied hard, learned English,	35
and became a scientist. In 1980, he was chosen by NASA to	47
become an astronaut. After six years of training, he had his first	59
flight on the space shuttle Columbia. His dream came true.	69
Franklin flew on seven space flights. After his flights, he	79
became a director at Johnson Space Center in Houston. He	89
retired from NASA in 2005. Now he is a physics professor.	100

With your partner, find the words that slowed you down.

• Practice saying each word and then say the sentence each word is in.

• Then take turns reading the text again. Count the number of words you read.

189

Taking Tests

You will often take tests that help show what you know.
Follow these tips to improve your test-taking skills.

Coaching Corner

Answering Questions About a Selection

- Many test questions ask you to answer questions about a selection.

- The selection can be fiction or nonfiction.

- The selection can be long or short.

- Before you read the selection, preview the questions and answer choices.

- After reading the selection, first try to answer each question in your head.

- Choose the answer that comes closest to the answer in your head.

- Check to make sure your answer choice is supported by the text.

Read the selection. Then answer the questions.

July 20, 1969, was the first day a man walked on the moon. The mission was called Apollo 11. Three astronauts traveled in a spaceship to reach the moon. They were Neil Armstrong, Michael Collins, and Edwin "Buzz" Aldrin. The main spaceship was the Columbia. It had a smaller ship inside. The smaller ship was the Eagle. The Eagle landed on the moon. Neil and Buzz walked on the moon. At the same time, Michael orbited the moon in the Columbia. When they all came back to Earth, they got a hero's welcome.

1 What was the name of the mission?

    A Apollo 11

    B Columbia

    C Eagle

    D Apollo 13

2 How many astronauts walked on the moon?

    F One

    G Two

    H Three

    J Four

3 Which is the best summary of this paragraph?

    A The life of Neil Armstrong

    B The day man first landed on the moon

    C The making of Apollo 11

    D Returning home to a hero's welcome

Tips

✓ Be careful. Two of the answer choices in Question 1 have the same word. The other two answer choices are also in the selection. Only one answer is correct.

✓ Make sure the answer you choose makes sense.

Art for Everyone

People celebrate and share art through festivals and public art displays.

Reading 1
Social Studies

Arts Festival!

Reading 2
Instructions

How to Make Puppets

Reading 3
Article

Painting for the Public

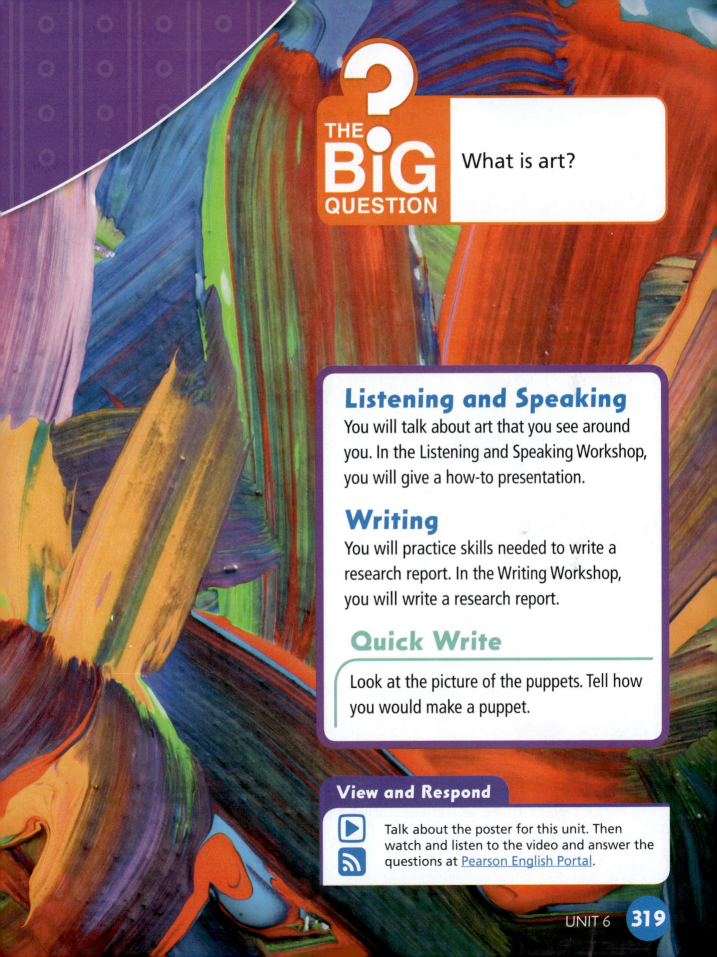

THE BiG QUESTION

What is art?

Listening and Speaking

You will talk about art that you see around you. In the Listening and Speaking Workshop, you will give a how-to presentation.

Writing

You will practice skills needed to write a research report. In the Writing Workshop, you will write a research report.

Quick Write

Look at the picture of the puppets. Tell how you would make a puppet.

View and Respond

Talk about the poster for this unit. Then watch and listen to the video and answer the questions at Pearson English Portal.

Words to Know

Listen and repeat. Use these words to talk about art.

 **puppets**

 **mask**

 **paper flowers**

 **mural**

 **vase**

Practice

Work with a partner. Ask and answer questions. Try to extend your conversation.

Example: A: Do you know how to make <u>puppets</u>?

B: No, I don't. Do you?

A: Yes, I do. I made <u>puppets</u> once in Mr. Kelly's class.

Write

Read the question. Write your response in your notebook.

Write two or three sentences about a piece of art you have in your home or your classroom. What does it look like?

Make Connections

Complete the sentences.

a sock

tissue paper

paintbrushes

paint

1. **A:** Look. I found this old _____ in my room.

   B: You should use it to make a puppet.

2. **A:** Let's paint our masks now.

   B: OK. I have paint, but we need two _____.

3. **A:** What can I make for my mom for her birthday?

   B: Let's use this _____ to make some paper flowers.

4. **A:** What happens if you mix black and white _____?

   B: The color becomes gray.

What about you?

Which of the things on page 320 do you know how to make? Tell your partner how to make it.

Kids' Stories from around the World 🎧

United Kingdom

U.S.A.

Stacey

I live in Tennessee, U.S.A. There is a big storytelling festival there. People come from all over to tell stories. The storytellers make us laugh. They tell tales about the past. Children can also tell stories at the festival.

Ben

I live in London, England. There is an artist here who paints pictures on buildings and sidewalks. No one knows who the artist is. We call him Banksy. His art is very interesting.

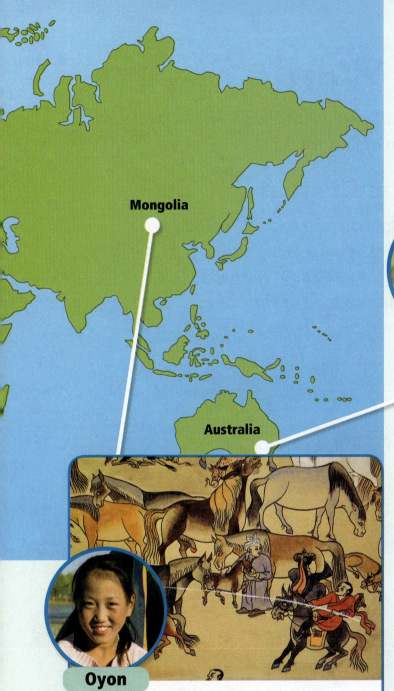

Mongolia

Australia

Aidan

I live in Australia. Every year there is an outdoor sculpture exhibition. It is on Bondi Beach. We go to see the different sculptures and art exhibits. There are over 70 art pieces to look at! At the festival, my sister bought a poster of her favorite sculpture.

Oyon

I live in Mongolia. Here, we think horses are very important. We celebrate horses in art. For the Rainbow Horse Festival, artists made 88 horse sculptures. Children painted the horse sculptures. It was a great festival.

What about you?

1. What kind of art do you like to make or see?

2. Do you have a story about a festival you have attended? Share your story.

Key Words

Arts Festival! tells about a big event in the town of Red Tree.

Words in Context

1 My neighborhood has a Cinco de Mayo **festival**. It is like a big party. We celebrate our Mexican history. There is delicious food, an art show, and great music.

What You Will Learn

Reading
- Vocabulary building: *Context, phonics*
- Reading strategy: *Identify author's purpose*
- Text type: *Informational text*
  - *poster*
  - *schedule*
  - *business letter*

Grammar
Commas

Writing
Plan a research report

These words will help you understand the reading.

Key Words

festival

advertise

schedule

supplies

2 This is a poster to **advertise** a dance festival at a school. People will see the poster and come to the festival.

3 This **schedule** tells what Class 3-A does each morning.

3

Class 3-A Morning Schedule

8:30–8:45 Morning Greeting

8:45–9:30 Science

9:30–10:15 Art

10:15–11:00 Math

11:00–12:00 Reading

12:00–12:45 Lunch

4 Here are some of my school **supplies**. I have pencils, a pencil sharpener, an eraser, and a ruler.

Practice

Make flashcards to help you memorize the words.
- Write a key word on the front.
- On the back, write the meaning.

Make Connections

What art do you like to make? Do you like to draw, dance, or sing? Tell what you would do at an arts **festival**.

193

These words will help you talk about the reading.

Academic Words

annual
happening every year

participate
be involved in

Academic Words

Words in Context

Our school has an **annual** election. Every year we choose a new class president.

Sometimes I **participate** in a discussion. Other times I just listen and don't say anything.

Practice

Choose an academic word to complete each sentence.

1. My family always goes to the _____ arts festival in my town.

2. If runners want to _____ in the race, they need to arrive early.

Apply

Ask and answer with a partner.

1. What is an **annual** event that you look forward to each year?

2. What school activity do you **participate** in?

Phonics

Diphthongs: *ou, ow*

A dipththong is a combination of two vowel sounds to make one vowel sound like **ou** in *house*. Read the words. Listen for the vowel sounds. Then read each word aloud.

ou	*ow*
out	how
sound	brown

Rule

Use *ou* at the beginning or in the middle of a word.
Use *ow* at the end of a word.

Practice

Work with a partner. Take turns.

- Read the sentences. Listen for words that have diphthongs.

- List words with *ou*; List words with *ow*.

- Add three more words to each list.

  1. How do you make a puppet?

  2. I will use this brown yarn.

  3. She drew a mouth on the face.

  4. Find out what you can do!

195

More About **THE BiG QUESTION**

Why is it important to advertise an arts festival?

🎧 **Listen to the Audio.**
First, listen for the main points.
Then listen again for important
details. Take notes as you listen.

Reading Strategy

Identify Author's Purpose

Authors write for different reasons.
As you read, look for the author's
purpose.

- An author may write to tell
  about something, or to get
  readers to do something.

- An author may write something
  for readers to enjoy.

Listen as your teacher models the
reading strategy.

Arts Festival!

by Rouenna Albright

The town of Red Tree has an
arts festival each year. It is called the
Summer Arts Festival. All the people
in the town come.

Children and **adults** can
take art classes. They can go to a
demonstration to learn how to make
pottery or a **collage**.

People work together to get ready for
the arts festival. One person makes a
poster. Another person makes a schedule.
Ms. Tan, the art teacher, writes a letter.

---

adults   fully grown people

demonstration   showing how to
do something

collage   picture made by attaching different
pictures onto a surface

Poster

This poster tells about the arts festival. It tells what day the festival is. It tells where the festival will be. The poster helps **advertise** the festival. People put up posters around Red Tree. Other people will see the posters. They will want to come to the festival.

Join your friends and neighbors at the festival.

Come to the Summer Arts Festival!

When? Saturday, June 3, 10 AM
Where? The Middle School Field and Gym
What? Art Activities for All Ages
AND The Great Puppet-Making Contest
Make your own puppet.
Win a prize.

Before You Go On

How does the poster help advertise the festival?

Business Letter

Ms. Tan writes a formal letter. In her letter, Ms. Tan asks for a **donation**.

———————————————————————

donation something someone gives

May 14, 2019

Ms. June Tan
Red Tree Arts Center
233 Ferry Road
Red Tree, CA 92688

Ms. Kay Cork
Cork Arts and Crafts
531 South Drive
Red Tree, CA 92688

Dear Ms. Cork,

The Summer Arts Festival will take place in June. This year, there will be a puppet-making contest. Anyone can enter.

I am writing to ask for your help. We need art supplies for making puppets. Specifically, we need colored paper, paste, crayons, and markers.

Many people in Red Tree come to the festival. Your donation would be a great way to advertise the store. It will also help the artists of Red Tree!

Thank you,

June Tan
Art Teacher

Summer Arts Festival

10:00	Morning Classes
	Painting
	Drawing
	Crafts
11:00	Pottery Demonstration
12:00	Family Painting Class
1:00	Afternoon Classes
	Painting
	Drawing
	Pottery
2:00	Collage Demonstration
3:00	Puppet-Making Contest
4:00	Art Show
	Prizes for Best Puppets

WB
196–198

Reading Strategy

Identify Author's Purpose

- Think about the poster, schedule, and letter. What was each author's purpose?

- How did looking for the author's purpose help you to understand?

Think It Over

1. **Recall** What is the annual arts festival called?

2. **Comprehend** What events can people participate in at the arts festival?

3. **Analyze** How do the poster, letter, and schedule contribute to the success of the arts festival?

Learning Strategies

Author's Purpose

Authors have different reasons for writing. Here are ways to find the **author's purpose**.

If the selection . . .		the author's purpose is to
tells about something,	→	inform.
tries to get the reader to do something,	→	persuade.
is written for the reader to enjoy,	→	entertain.

Practice

Think about the parts of *Arts Festival*! Tell if the author's purpose is to inform, persuade, or entertain.

1. The Summer Arts Festival poster
2. The Summer Arts Festival schedule
3. June Tan's formal letter

Use a T-Chart

You can use a T-Chart to show the author's purpose.

Practice

First, write the author's purpose for each type of text. Then read paragraphs 1, 2, and 3 below. What is the author's purpose for each paragraph? Write it in the chart.

Selection	Author's Purpose
poster	inform
schedule	
formal letter	
Paragraph 1	
Paragraph 2	
Paragraph 3	

1. Larry hopped into the room. It was his first day. The children looked at him. Some of them laughed. Larry did not care. He was happy to be the first rabbit to take art class.

2. We should have art classes in school every day. Researchers say that students who participate three or four times a week in art activities perform better in their other subjects.

3. Painting is an old form of art. People have used paints for more than 20,000 years. The first paintings were in a cave.

199

Apply

Summarize the selection "Arts Festival" for a partner.

Extension

Discuss with a partner:
What are the benefits of art classes in school?

Grammar

Commas

Commas (,) are used to separate words, phrases, or clauses.
They can make writing clearer and easier to understand.

Study these common uses of the comma.

DATES
- between the day of the week and the date: Saturday, June 3
- between the date and the year: May 14, 2019

LOCATIONS
- between the city and state or province or country in sentences:
    I lived in La Plata, Buenos Aires, Argentina.

LETTERS
- after the greeting: Dear June, / Hi, Lola
- after the closing: Thank you, / Sincerely,

SERIES (a series consists of three or more items)
- between all items:
    We need colored paper, paste, crayons, and markers.

CLAUSES
- before *and* or *but* in a compound sentence
    She talked, and he listened.
    She talked, but he didn't listen.

Practice A

Add commas where needed. Write the sentences in your notebook.

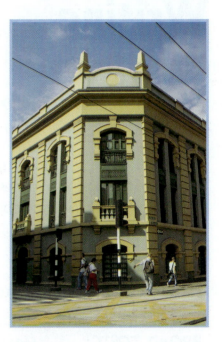

1. He comes from Medellin Colombia.

   He comes from Medellin, Colombia.

2. He will arrive on Tuesday November 7.

3. I saw Rick Donna and Linda at the party.

4. My cousins live in Manchester England.

5. Where were you on May 13 2018?

6. We ate oranges figs grapes and bananas.

Practice B

Read the questions in Apply. Write your answers to the questions in your notebook. Use commas where needed.

Apply

Work with a partner. Using your answers in Practice B, take turns asking and answering the questions.

Example: A: What city and state or province do you live in?

B: I live in Jakarta, Indonesia.

- What three things do you like to do?
- What are your three favorite television shows?
- What month, day, and year were you born?
- What four foods do you like to eat?

> **Grammar Check** ✔
>
> Write a sentence that includes a **series**. Use **commas** correctly.

200

Writing

Plan a Research Report

In a research report, you explain a topic that you have studied.

> ### Task 1
>
> First, choose a topic. What interests you? What would you like to learn more about? List a topic in a graphic organizer. Then write some questions and answers about the topic.

A student named Elissa listed her ideas in this chart:

BROAD TOPIC:	Mexican artists
QUESTION:	Who are some famous Mexican artists?
ANSWER:	Frida Kahlo and Diego Rivera
QUESTION:	Why is Frida Kahlo famous?
ANSWER:	She painted brightly colored pictures with images of her country.

Elissa decided to write her report about her second question, "Why is Frida Kahlo famous?"

Write a Research Question

Next, Elissa made a list of questions about Frida Kahlo.

1. When was Frida Kahlo born?
2. How did Frida Kahlo's life affect her art?
3. What is Frida Kahlo's most famous painting?

Task 2

Study your list of questions. Then choose the question that interests you most. This question will direct the research for your report.

Make a Research Plan

Elissa chose question number 2 as the topic for her report. To create a research plan, she made a list of things she wanted to know about this topic. She listed them in a T-Chart:

What do I want to know?	Where can I find this information?
1. What was Frida Kahlo's early life like?	Website http://www. biographiesforkids.org/bios/ frida-kahlo
2. How did Frida Kahlo feel about her art?	Book: Fabiny, Sarah. *Who was Frida Kahlo?*, New York, New York: Penguin, 2013. Print.
3. What were Frida Kahlo's paintings like?	Leveton, Deborah. "Frida Kahlo." *World Book Encyclopedia.* Chicago: World Book, Inc., 2017. 209. Print.

Task 3

Create a research plan. Make a list of what you want to learn and where to look for it. Use a T-Chart.

What You Will Learn

Reading

- Vocabulary building: *Context, phonics*
- Reading strategy: *Identify steps in a process*
- Text type: *Informational Text (instructions)*

Grammar
The imperative

Writing
How to write a paraphrase

These words will help you understand the reading.

Key Words

puppets

scissors

stapler

yarn

buttons

Key Words

How to Make Puppets tells how to make a puppet.

Words in Context

1 **Puppets** can be big or small. Some you move with strings. Some can fit on your fingers.

2 Some **scissors** cut paper. Other scissors cut cloth.

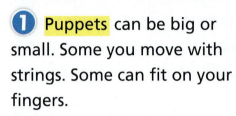

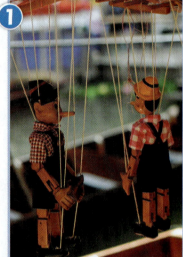

3 A <mark>stapler</mark> is a useful tool. This boy staples pieces of paper.

4 They are knitting with <mark>yarn</mark>. The grandmother helps the girl.

5 <mark>Buttons</mark> come in many shapes and sizes. Would you like these buttons on a shirt?

Practice

Draw pictures of the key words. Label each picture with a sentence that contains the key word.

Make Connections

Do you like to make crafts? What would you make with yarn, buttons, and cloth?

203

These words will help you talk about the reading.

Academic Words

required
something needed

reverse
backward; opposite way

Academic Words

Words in Context

All that is **required** for tomorrow's exam is a pencil and an eraser.

When you make a question with *be,* you **reverse** the order of the subject and verb.

Practice

Choose an academic word to complete each sentence.

1. Before making a birdhouse, gather together all of the parts that are _____.

2. My brother's name in _____ is M-A-S.

Apply

Ask and answer with a partner.

1. What kind of clothing is **required** for a trip to a very cold place?

2. Can you say the alphabet in **reverse**, starting with *z*? Try it.

Phonics 🎧

The Letter Y

The letter *y* can be a vowel. It can be a consonant, too.

Rule

The letter *y* may have a long *e* sound at the end of the word.
The letter *y* may have a long *i* sound at the end of the word.
The letter *y* may be a consonant when it is at the start of a word or syllable.

Listen. Then read each word aloud.

Vowel: long *e*	Vowel: long *i*	Consonant
city	my	you
party	try	yes
busy		

Practice

Work with a partner. Take turns.

- Read the words in the chart. Listen for the sounds of the letter *y*.
- Add four words to each column.

205

Informational Text
Instructions

Why is it important to read directions to make a craft?

🎧 **Listen to the Audio.**
First, listen for the main points. Then listen again for important details. Take notes as you listen.

Reading Strategy

Identify Steps in a Process

Identifying the steps in a process can help you understand how information is connected.

- Look at the pictures.
- Pay attention to the order of the steps for making a puppet.

Listen as your teacher models the reading strategy.

How to Make Puppets

by Pravina Cole

People have been making puppets for thousands of years. Children like to play with puppets. People can use puppets to tell stories, too.

Do you know how to make a puppet? You can learn. Read the directions. First, you need to **gather** the supplies.

---

gather get things and put them together

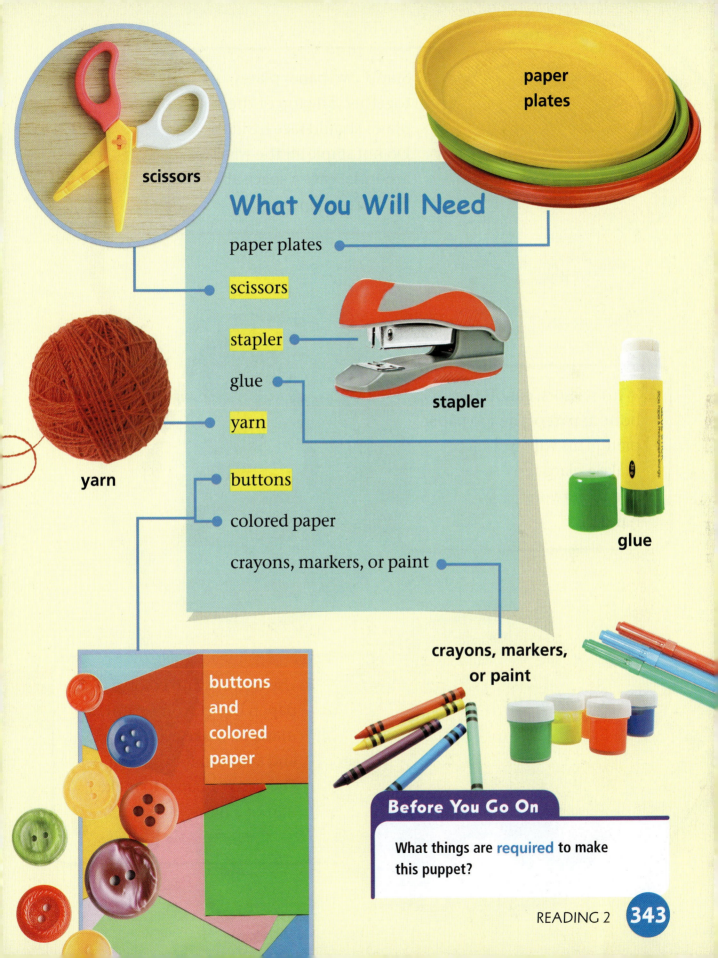

scissors

paper plates

What You Will Need

paper plates

scissors

stapler

glue

yarn

buttons

colored paper

crayons, markers, or paint

stapler

glue

yarn

crayons, markers, or paint

buttons and colored paper

Before You Go On

What things are **required** to make this puppet?

1. Staple two paper plates together. The top of the plates should face inside. Do not staple all the way around. Leave a space at the bottom open.

2. With scissors, cut off the bottom part of the top paper plate. This will make a place for you to put your hand.

3. Use buttons and colored paper. Use crayons, paint, or markers. Make eyes, a nose, and a mouth for your puppet. Use yarn or paper to make hair or a hat.

4. Now you have made a puppet. Put your hand inside the space between the two paper plates. You can move the puppet by moving your hand.

Can you make your puppet talk? What will it say?

Use your puppet to put on a show or to tell a story.

206–208

Reading Strategy

Identify Steps in a Process

- What are the steps for making a puppet?

- Did identifying the order of the steps help you understand the selection? How?

Think It Over

1. **Recall** Which step explains how to make the puppet's face?

2. **Comprehend** How do you make a place to hold the puppet?

3. **Analyze** What would happen if you **reversed** the order of steps 1–3? Would the process still work?

Puppets

▲ **Puppeteer**

The person who works a puppet is a puppeteer. This puppeteer and puppet are in India.

▲ **Sock puppet**

A sock puppet is easy to make. You just need a clean sock and some buttons.

▲ **Shadow puppets**

This is a shadow puppet show in Malaysia. Can you see the sticks? Puppeteers use the sticks to move the puppets.

▲ Behind the stage

These puppeteers watch their puppets on a video screen. They can see the stage during the show.

▲ Marionette

Marionettes are puppets that hang from strings. When the puppeteer moves the strings, the puppet moves.

▲ Puppets that teach

This teacher is using a dinosaur puppet to help his students learn.

Activity to Do

These two pages use pictures and words to tell about puppets.

- Choose another toy.
- Find pictures to show that toy.
- Post your pictures and captions in your classroom.

Learning Strategies

Reread for Details

If you do not understand the selection the first time you read it, read the selection again. You may also find new information the second time you read it.

Practice

Look back in the selection for the answers to these questions. Tell the page number you found the answer on.

1. What can people use puppets to do?
2. What supplies do you need?
3. After you staple the two paper plates together, what's the next step?
4. When the puppet is finished, how can you move it?

Use a Sequence Chart

To make a puppet, you have to follow the steps in the right order.

 GO 4

Practice

Complete this Sequence Chart. List the steps given below in the right order.

- Cut off the bottom part of the top paper plate. This will make a place for you to put your hand.
- Place your hand inside the space between the two paper plates. You can move the puppet by moving your hand.
- Staple the paper plates together around the edges. Leave a space at the bottom open.
- Make eyes, a nose, and a mouth for your puppet. Add hair or a hat.

Apply

**Reread the selection and take notes.
Then close your book and retell the selection to a partner.**

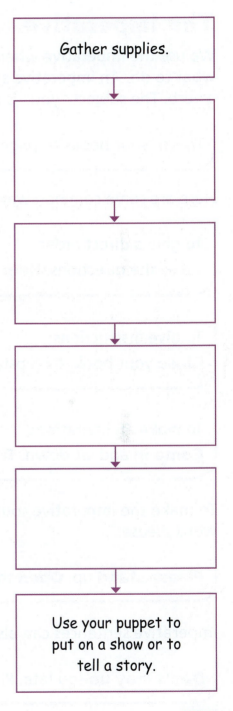

Gather supplies.

Use your puppet to put on a show or to tell a story.

Grammar

The Imperative

We use the **imperative** when we want to tell someone what to do. An imperative sentence usually begins with a verb. The subject "you" is implied.

Open your books to page 350.

Here are some common ways the imperative is used:

To give a direct order:
Read the directions. **Help** your brother.

To give instructions:
Close your book. **Go** upstairs and turn right.

To make an invitation:
Come in and **sit** down. **Try** one of these cookies.

To make the imperative sound more polite, add the word *please:*

Please **stand** up. **Open** the window, *please*.

Imperative sentences can also be negative:

Don't stay up too late. Please **don't forget** to call.

Practice A

Change each question into an imperative. In your notebook, write the sentences in order.

1. Will you come up to the stage with your marionette?
   Come up to the stage with your marionette.

2. Can you sing the song and make the marionette dance?

3. Will you stand in the middle of the stage?

4. Will you bow with the marionette after the performance?

5. Will you introduce yourself?

6. Will you hold up the marionette?

Practice B

Make two of the imperatives in Practice A more polite. Give your partner the commands. Switch roles.

Apply

Work with a partner. Choose one of the questions below and write instructions. Use imperative sentences. Then tell your instructions to your partner.

Example: A: How do you make a sandwich?

B: First, see what is in the refrigerator. Next,...

- How do you play soccer?
- How do you make a bed?
- How do you make breakfast?
- How do you draw a picture?
- How do you play tag?

> **Grammar Check** ✔
>
> Write two **imperative** sentences: one affirmative, and one negative.

210

Writing

How to Write a Paraphrase

One way to support your ideas in a research report is to put the information you find into your own words. This is called **paraphrasing.**

Task

Find information about an art form, such as photography or painting, or about a favorite artist. Then paraphrase this information in your own words. List your ideas in a graphic organizer. Give information about your source.

A student named Elissa listed her ideas in this chart.

Information from Text
• had polio when she was six
• the disease made her right leg weak
• in a bus accident when she was 18
• began to paint while in bed
Paraphrase of Information
When she was six, she had polio. This made one of her legs weak. When she was 18, she was in a bad bus accident. She couldn't leave her bed, but she began to paint again.
Research Source
"Frida Kahlo," *Biographies for Kids*. December 20, 2017, http://www.biographiesforkids.org/bios/frida-kahlo.

Writing Information about a Source

When Elissa wrote her description of her research source, she included the following information:

- the name of the article "Frida Kahlo"
- the name of the website *Biographies for Kids*
- the date she found the information (December 20, 2017)
- the address of the website (http://www.biographiesforkids.org/bios/frida-kahlo)

Here is part of Elissa's Research Report. It is based on the paraphrase she wrote.

> Elissa Chen
>
> Frida Kahlo had many difficult times in her life. When she was six years old, she became ill with a serious disease called polio. This made one of her legs weaker than the other. When she was 18, she was in a terrible bus accident. It took her a long time to get better. Even though she couldn't leave her bed, she continued to paint.
>
> Works Consulted List
>
> "Frida Kahlo." *Biographies for Kids*. 20 December 2017. <http://www.biographiesforkids.org/bios/frida-kahlo>

Key Words

Painting for the Public is about people who create public art for everyone to see.

Words in Context

1 Marco can **create** animals by folding pieces of paper.

2 Mr. Lee's class drew with chalk on a **public** sidewalk.

3 The artist painted a dove as a **statement** of peace.

4 Sarah raised money for a book drive, a **cause** that is important to her.

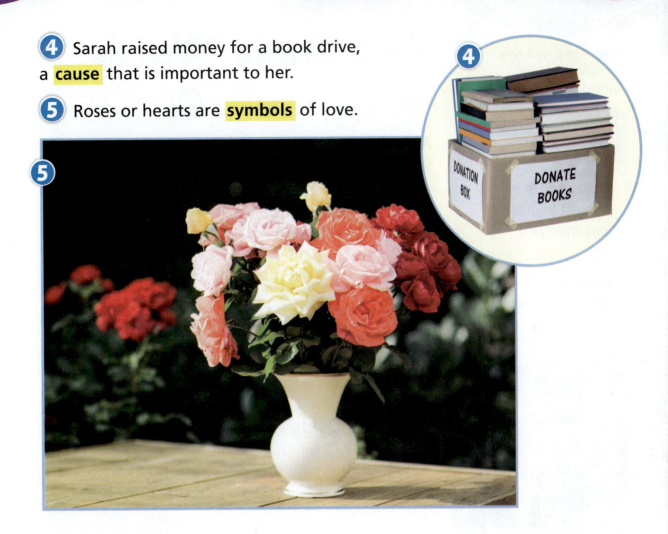

5 Roses or hearts are **symbols** of love.

Practice

Add a page to your vocabulary notebook.

- Divide your page into three columns: the new words, their definitions, and drawings of the words when possible.
- Test yourself by covering one of the columns.

Make Connections

Which do you like better: creating art or looking at art at an art festival or in a museum?

213

These words will help you talk about the reading.

Academic Words

alternative
different from something else

goal
something you want to achieve

Academic Words

Words in Context

At home we have many **alternative** activities besides watching TV.

Al's **goal** was to read two more books before the end of summer.

Practice

Choose an academic word to complete each sentence.

1. My _____ for this year is to learn how to play chess.

2. The road is closed. We have to find an _____ way to get to the store.

Apply

Ask and answer with a partner.

1. How do you spell and pronounce your name? What is an **alternative** way to spell or pronounce your name?

2. What is one of your **goals** for the next week? What is one of your **goals** for the next 24 hours?

Word Study
Multi-Syllable Words

Read the words in the chart.

1 Syllable	2 Syllables	3 Syllables
goal	lead/er	af/ter/noon
my	out/door	beau/ti/ful
booths	trum/pet	Sat/ur/day

Rule

Each syllable has one vowel sound. The vowel sound may be spelled with more than one vowel letter.

Practice

Work with a partner. Make a chart with three columns like the one above.

• Write each word below in the correct column.

• Add two new words to each column.

art	painting	public	culture
celebrate	attention	paint	

Informational Text
Newspaper Article

More About THE BiG QUESTION

What types of art can you see in public?

🎧 Listen to the Audio.

First, listen for the main points. Then listen again for the important details. Take notes as you listen.

Reading Strategy

Draw Conclusions

To draw a conclusion from what you read, put together details from the selection.

- What types of art can people see in public?

- What do people think about public art?

- What can you conclude about the people who create public art?

Listen as your teacher models the reading strategy.

Painting for the Public

Public Paintings

You create paintings in art class. You've seen colorful paintings on walls in homes, offices, and other buildings. Maybe you've seen paintings in a museum. But have you ever seen paintings that cover the entire side of a building? Works of art you see outdoors in your community are called public art.

History of Public Art

Artists have been creating public art for a long time. Some people believe ancient drawings found on cave walls may have been the first pieces of public art.

Much later, in the 1960s and 1970s, **graffiti** became popular in cities. Most graffiti included a single word on the side of a building or a train car. Over time, it developed into something more. Public art is created on surfaces in public places such as sidewalks, sides of buildings, and other places. Today, public artists create public art for everyone to see.

---

graffiti   words or pictures painted on a wall in public place

Before You Go On

Why do artists create public art?

Why Public Art?

Every artist creates for a reason. Public artists are no different. Some want to make a ==statement== about an important ==cause== or problem, such as food insecurity or pollution. When artists create art in a wide-open public place, their message reaches more people. Ginnie Dickinson enjoys looking at the public art in her neighborhood. "There are so many different types of art to see," she said. "And I like looking at it when I walk to school with my dad." Ginnie's dad agrees. "The paintings are so colorful and interesting. Ginnie and I talk about what each one means."

Other artists create public art to celebrate a community or culture. Still other artists want to make a rundown empty space more lively and beautiful.

Public Artists Around the World

Public art is in cities all over the world. Here are some examples.

Mona Caron is an artist in San Francisco. She paints murals and illustrations on the sides of buildings and in her studio. She is best known for her murals of huge plants on the sides of buildings. More specifically, she paints weeds, which are plants people usually step on or simply don't notice. "The less people pay attention to it," Caron says, "the larger I'm going to paint it!" When asked why she paints weeds, she says, "Any little bit of nature is actually incredibly beautiful if you take the time to look at it."

Mona believes in using art to help people and bring awareness to important issues. Her art has been used to support climate awareness, water rights, and groups that want to help workers around the world.

Before You Go On

What **alternative** way does Canon display her art?

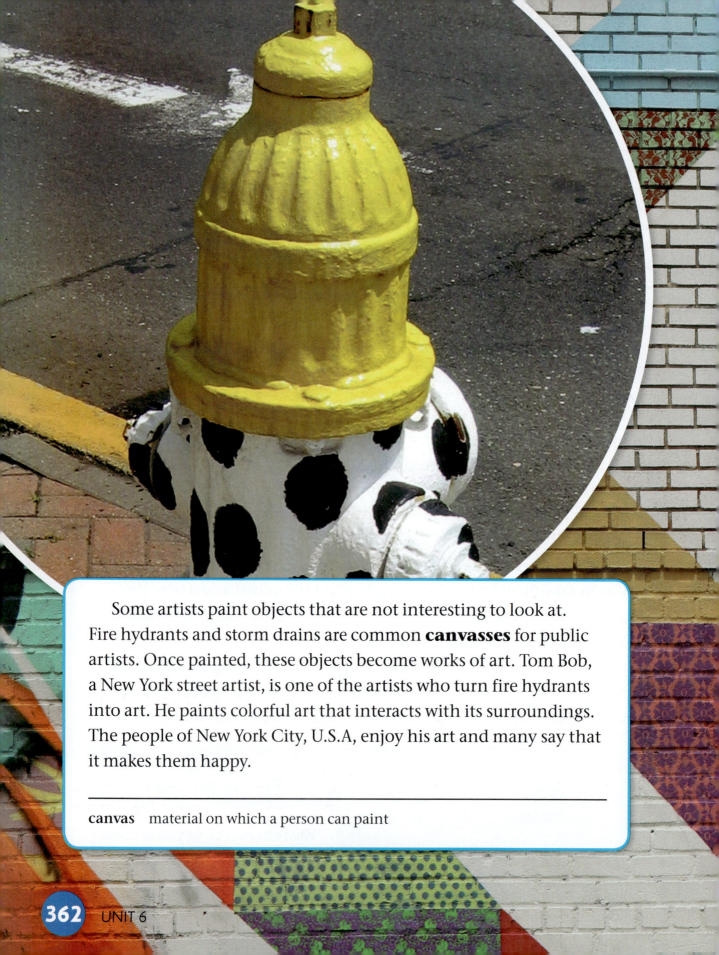

Some artists paint objects that are not interesting to look at. Fire hydrants and storm drains are common **canvasses** for public artists. Once painted, these objects become works of art. Tom Bob, a New York street artist, is one of the artists who turn fire hydrants into art. He paints colorful art that interacts with its surroundings. The people of New York City, U.S.A, enjoy his art and many say that it makes them happy.

---

canvas   material on which a person can paint

Brazilian Alex Senna is another public artist. He is color-blind, which means that he cannot see all colors. When he first started painting, he used one color in his drawings and sketchbooks. He then started painting city walls. His paintings are unique because he uses only black-and-white paint.

Senna taught himself how to draw. He uses comic books to help him become a better artist. Most of his murals can be found on the sides of buildings in São Paulo, Brazil. They look a bit like cartoons. Senna often includes ==symbols== such as hearts, balloons, and birds in his murals. His paintings are meant to be messages of love and romance. These are messages that everyday people can relate to and understand.

Next time you are out in your community, look for public art. Then find out more about it!

W B
216–218

Think It Over

1. **Recall** What is the **goal** of Caron's paintings?

2. **Comprehend** What are some ways that public artists make ==statements==?

3. **Analyze** Why would viewing public art be a fun activity for a family to do together?

Reading Strategy

Draw Conclusions

- What can you conclude about how people feel when they see Alex Senna's murals?

- What details in the selection helped you reach this conclusion?

Learning Strategies

Draw a Conclusion

To **draw a conclusion**, use details from the selection to make your own ideas. The 5 W questions can help you identify important details. The 5 W questions are *who, what, where, when,* and *why.*

Answer the questions. Draw a conclusion about the reasons people create public art.

1. Who creates public art?
2. Why do artists create public art? What do you think the main reason is?
3. What types of art do public artists create?
4. What are some additional reasons artists create public art? Explain how you reached the conclusion.

Use a 5 W Chart

Use a 5 W Chart to ask questions about the article *Painting for the Public*.

GO 6

Practice

Copy the chart. Use your answers to draw a conclusion about public art and artists.

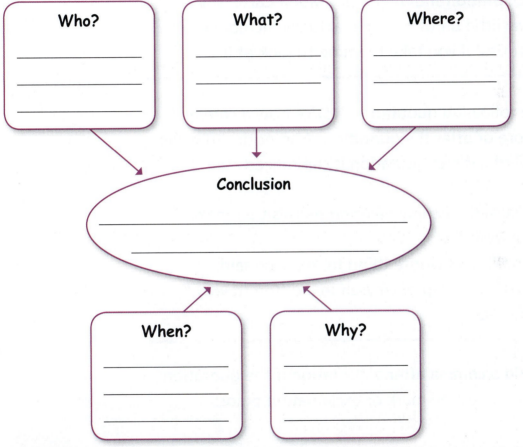

Who?	What?	Where?

Conclusion

When?	Why?

WB
219

Apply

Summarize the selection. Use some of the key words as you speak.

Extension

Work with a partner. Find a picture of a mural that you like. Share your finding with the class.

Grammar

Quotations

A **direct quotation** shows a speaker's **exact words**. **Quotation marks (" ")** show a reader where the spoken words begin and end.

> **Direct Quotation showing what Mona Caron says:**
> "Any little bit of nature is actually incredibly beautiful if you take the time to look at it."

Read the following quotations. Notice how a **comma** is used before or after the quotation. Also notice that the first word of a direct quotation is capitalized.

> The artist said, "I enjoy painting murals that make people happy."
> "Creating is my favorite thing to do," she said.
> "It allows me to express myself in a different way," she continued.

Do not add a comma after a quotation if the quotation ends with a question mark or exclamation point:

> "Can we go see the new sculptures?" asked Emma.
> "I want to be an artist someday!" Emma exclaimed.

Add quotation marks to show exactly what words the person said. Use commas correctly.

1. He said You did great!
   He said, "You did great!"

2. I love those musicians said Anita.

3. Me, too! exclaimed her friend.

4. This is a great festival added Tony.

5. Anita said Are all artists this good?

6. My **goal** is to be like them Tony said.

Practice B

Read the conversation in Apply. Copy it in your notebook. Put commas and quotation marks where needed.

Apply

Work with a partner. Decide who will read Carol's and Jaimie's parts. Take turns reading the lines out loud. Read with expression.

- Hey said Jaimie where are you going?
- To the arts festival Carol replied.
- Can I go with you? asked Jaimie.
- If you have a ticket Carol said sure. But hurry up.
- Can I get my ticket at the entrance? asked Jaimie.
- Yes, of course Carol said. Walk faster!
- Oh no! Carol exclaimed. Where's everybody?
- Look at the sign! Jaimie said. The festival was yesterday!

> **Grammar Check ✔**
>
> Give an example of a **direct quotation**.

220

Writing

How to Use Quotations

In addition to paraphrasing, another way to support your ideas in a research report is to use **quotations**. A quote is what other people have said or have written about your topic. You can find quotations for your research report from different sources, including books, magazines, and websites.

After the quotation you must also include information about the source of the quote. Put the author's name or the name of the website in parentheses at the end of the quotation.

Task

Find research information about an art form, such as photography or painting, or about an artist that you like. Include at least one quotation from a research source. Put quotation marks around the words you use. List your ideas in a graphic organizer.

A student named Elissa listed her ideas in this chart:

QUOTATION	"Viva la vida!" In English, that means "Long live life!"
SOURCE	Fabiny, Sarah. *Who Was Frida Kahlo?*, New York, New York: Penguin, 2013. Print.

Writing Information about a Source

When Elissa wrote her description of her research source, she included the following information:

- the name of the author (Sarah Fabiny)
- the name of the book (*Who Was Frida Kahlo?*)
- the location and name of the publisher (New York: Penguin Group)
- the year the book was published (2013)

Here is part of Elissa's Research Report. It includes the quotation from the book. At the end of the quotation, she included a citation for the quote. The citation is the author of the book's last name and the page number where she found the quote.

Elissa Chen

Although she suffered many difficulties in her lifetime, Kahlo never lost her love for life. "Viva la vida!" In English, that means "Long live life!" (Fabiny 1)

Works Consulted List

Fabiny, Sarah. *Who Was Frida Kahlo?*, New York, New York: Penguin, 2013. Print.

Apply and Extend

Link the Readings

Read the words in the top row of the chart.

- For *Arts Festival!,* put an X under the words that remind you of the selection.

- Repeat the same activity for the other readings.

	Informational text	Literature	Making art	Annual event
Arts Festival!				
How to Make Puppets				
Painting for the Public				

Discussion

1. In *Arts Festival!,* how do people prepare for the **annual** festival? How do they **participate** in it?

2. How are the festivals described in this unit similar? How are they different?

3. What different kinds of art are mentioned in the three readings?

THE BiG QUESTION What is art?

Listening Skills

If you want to confirm your understanding, you can say, "Do you mean...?

Projects

Your teacher will help you choose one of these projects.

Written	Oral	Visual/Active
Newspaper Article Write a short article about public art for your school newspaper. Describe what it is and say why people should look for public art around their community.	**Group Plan** Work with a group. Plan an arts festival at your school. Make a schedule for the event. Give a formal presentation of the plan to your class.	**Advertising Poster** Make a poster to advertise an arts festival. Answer the 5 W questions in your poster.
Journal/Blog Write a blog about public art. Describe the types of public art, such as graffiti and murals, you have seen in your community. Describe your own feelings about the public art that you have seen.	**Artist Interview** Interview an artist in your community. Ask about what the artist has made and shown. Make a list of questions. Then tell the class about the artist's work.	**Festival Collage** Find photos of artwork on the internet or in magazines. Make a collage of all different kinds of art that might be displayed at an arts festival.

 For more resources, visit **Pearson English Portal**

223–224

Listening and Speaking Workshop
Give a How-to Presentation

You are going to write and give a how-to presentation. Then you will listen as your classmates present their how-to presentations.

① Prepare

A. Choose a recipe, a craft, or a game. You will present how to do it to your classmates. Then your classmates will ask you questions.

B. Think about the different steps. Then write your how-to presentation. Remember to describe what you are going to demonstrate, and then explain each step. Find props to use in the presentation.

> Today I'm going to show you how to take good photos with a digital camera. There are several ways to make your pictures better.
>
> First, learn how to use your camera correctly. Then, take pictures of objects in different ways. Get up high or get close to the object. Next, make sure the background is interesting. Then, you want to hold the camera straight so the picture is not fuzzy....

② Practice

Find a partner. Practice your presentation in front of your partner. Your partner will act out or mime your instructions. Work with your partner to improve your presentation. Switch roles.

Useful Language

 Listen and repeat.

Today I'm going to show you how to . . .

It's really easy.

You need . . .

First, . . .

Next, . . .

Remember to . . .

③ Present

As you speak, do the following:

- Speak clearly and slowly.
- Show your props or other visuals.
- After your presentation, answer your classmates' questions.

As you listen, do the following:

- Listen for each step and take notes.
- Listen for ideas and information that is not stated directly.
- Think of questions to ask the speaker after the presentation.

④ Evaluate

After you speak, answer these questions:

✔ Did you explain each step?

✔ Did working with your partner help you?

After you listen, answer these questions:

✔ Was the presentation formal or informal?

✔ Did you take notes?

✔ Did you ask any questions?

✔ Did the instructions make sense? Would you be able to explain the steps to someone else?

✔ Think about the general meaning of the presentation. Can you think of a title for it? Tell your idea to the class.

Writing Workshop
Write a Research Report

Writing Prompt

Write a research report that you began earlier in this unit. Present a main idea, and include facts and details to support it. Gather information from a variety of sources such as books, magazines, or online websites.

① Prewrite

Review the lessons in this unit. You have chosen and narrowed a topic. You have created a research plan. You have learned to paraphrase and quote directly from your sources.

A. Taking Notes

Now it is time to do your research. As you research your topic, take notes on note cards. Use one note card for each idea. Follow these steps:

- Write a label for the idea at the top of the card.
- Write your paraphrase or your quotation in the body of the card.
- Write the source, author, publisher, and page number at the bottom of the card.

You will use your cards when you plan your outline and write your report.

Here is an example of a note card:

> ### Important Milestones in Frida Kahlo's Life
>
> 1. Born in 1907 in Coyoacán, Mexico
> 2. Became ill with polio when she was six
> 3. Had a serious bus accident when she was 18
> 4. Married Mexican painter, Diego Rivera, in 1929
> Source: "Frida Kahlo," *Biographies for Kids*. December 20, 2017,
> http://www.biographiesforkids.org/bios/frida-kahlo.

B. Making an Outline

Decide what order you would like to present the ideas in your report. Refer to your notecards. When you are ready, create an outline.

> ### The Life of Frida Kahlo
>
> A. Introduction
>   1. One of world's great artists
>   2. Painted colorful images from Mexico
>   3. Work still very popular today
> B. Frida Kahlo's life
>   1. Born in 1907, Coyoacán, Mexico
>   2. Married Diego Rivera, a famous painter
> C. Her illness and accident
>   1. Contracted polio when she was six years old
>   2. Terrible bus accident when she was 18
> D. Conclusion
>   1. Kahlo's work showed her love for Mexico
>   2. Never stopped painting; her story inspires others

② Draft

Use your outline to help you write a first draft.

- Begin with a paragraph that clearly presents your topic.
- Use transition words to keep your ideas flowing smoothly.
- Include citations for paraphrases and quotations.

Citing Sources Use the following examples as models to help you cite your sources correctly:

Book Stewart, Amy. *Wicked Bugs*. North Carolina: Algonquin Young Readers, 2017. Print.

Magazine Article Humecke, Mary. "Tagging Monarch Butterflies." *Fun for Kidz*. May-June 2018: 12. Print.

Internet Website "Cool Jobs: Diving for New Medicine." Science News for Kids. 3 May 2018. <https://www.sciencenewsforstudents.org/article/cool-jobs-diving-new-medicines>

Encyclopedia Article Leveton, Deborah. "Frida Kahlo." *World Book Encyclopedia*. Chicago: World Book, Inc., 2017. 209. Print.

③ Revise

Read your draft. Look for places where the writing needs improvement. Use the Writing Checklist to help you. Then revise your draft.

Six Traits of Writing Checklist

✔ **Ideas**
Did my sentences relate to the topic?

✔ **Organization**
Did I support my writing with facts?

✔ **Voice**
Did my writing show my interest in the topic?

✔ **Word Choice**
Did I choose exact and interesting words?

✔ **Sentence Fluency**
Did I vary my sentences?

✔ **Conventions**
Did my writing follow the rules of grammar, punctuation, usage, and mechanics?

Here is how Elissa revised her research report:

Elissa Chen

Frida Kahlo, Artist

Frida Kahlo was one of the world's greatest artists. She painted pictures with bright colors and images from her country, Mexico. We still enjoy her art today.

Frida Kahlo was born in 1907. *, and she* She grew up in Mexico. When she was twenty-one years old, she met another famous Mexican painter named Diego Rivera. They were married in 1929. They both loved Mexican art and culture.

Frida Kahlo had many difficult times in her life. When she was six years old, she became ill with a serious disease called polio. This made one of her legs *a* weeker than the other. When she was 18, she was in a terrible bus accident. She had to stay in bed all the time, but she didn't stop painting.

Frida Kahlo's work showed her love for her country. *It also showed her determination.* Although she suffered many difficulties in her lifetime, she never lost her love for life. "Viva la vida!" In English, that means "Long live life!" (Fabiny 1) Frida Kahlo's story has inspired people to work hard at the things they love.

Revised to add apostrophe to show possession.

Revised to add transition word.

Revised to correct spelling error.

Revised to connect ideas.

Works Consulted List

"Frida Kahlo," *Biographies for Kids*. December 20, 2017,
    http://www.biographiesforkids.org/bios/frida-kahlo.

Fabiny, Sarah. *Who was Frida Kahlo?*, New York, New York:
    Penguin, 2013. Print.

Leveton, Deborah. "Frida Kahlo." *World Book Encyclopedia*.
    Chicago: World Book, Inc., 2017. 209. Print.

④ Edit

Check your work for errors. Trade papers with a partner. Use the Peer Review Checklist to give each other feedback.

⑤ Publish

Prepare a clean copy of your final draft. Share your essay with the class.

Peer Review Checklist

- ✓ The main ideas and details are clear.
- ✓ All the information is related to the topic.
- ✓ Quotes are used properly.

Fluency

Listen to the sentences. Pay attention to the groups of words. Read aloud.

1. The people of Red Tree work together to get ready for the arts festival.

2. People have made puppets for thousands of years, and you can too.

3. Public artists create public art for everyone to see.

Work in pairs. Take turns reading the text below aloud for one minute. Count the number of words you read.

Brazilian Alex Senna is another public artist. He is color-blind, which	11
means that he cannot see all colors. When he first started painting, he used	25
one color in his drawings and sketchbooks. He then started painting city	37
walls. His paintings are unique because he uses only black-and-white paint.	50
Senna taught himself how to draw. He uses comic books to help him	63
become a better artist. Most of his murals can be found on the sides of	78
buildings in São Paulo, Brazil. They look a bit like cartoons. Senna often	91
includes symbols such as hearts, balloons, and birds in his murals. His	103
paintings are meant to be messages of love and romance. These are messages	116
that everyday people can relate to and understand.	124

With your partner, find the words that slowed you down.

*   Practice saying each word and then say the sentence each word is in.

*   Then take turns reading the text again. Count the number of words you read.

227

Taking Tests

You will often take tests that help show what you know.
Follow these tips to improve your test-taking skills.

Coaching Corner

Answering Test Items That Are Cloze Items

- Cloze items ask you to fill in a blank.

- If there is a graphic, make sure you understand it.

- Read the questions and answer choices. Sometimes there is no question, just a list of words.

- Read the whole selection carefully. Try to think of words that might fit as you read.

- If you don't know what a word means, use the words around it to help you.

- In your head, read the sentence with each answer choice. Try each answer choice before choosing your answer. Choose the answer that makes the most sense.

Read the selection. Then choose the correct words to fill in the blanks.

It's fun to make after-school ___1___. These banana pops are easy and healthy. Make sure an adult helps you!

Ingredients for Banana Pops	
• 1 cup yogurt • ½ cup orange juice • 1 medium ripe banana, cut into pieces	• 6 small paper cups • blender

Have an adult help you measure the yogurt and juice. Have the adult cut the banana. Then put all the ___2___ into a blender. Mix until smooth. Next, pour the mixture into the paper cups. Put the cups in the freezer for about 5 hours. For more variety, try using other kinds of ___3___ instead of bananas. Makes 6 servings.

1 **A** homework

    B snacks

    C movies

    D juice

2 **F** chocolate

    G dishes

    H ingredients

    J bananas

3 **A** fruit

    B potatoes

    C bananas

    D pasta

Tips

 Be careful. Read the selection carefully.

 Try each answer choice in the blank. Choose the one that makes the most sense.

Study Skills and Language Learning

How to Learn Language

Learning a language involves listening, speaking, reading, and writing. You can use these tips to make the most of your language learning.

Listening

1. Listen with a purpose.
2. Listen actively.
3. Take notes.
4. Listen to speakers on the radio, television, and internet.

Speaking

1. Think before you speak.
2. Speak appropriately for your audience.
3. Practice reading aloud to a partner.
4. Practice speaking with friends and family members.
5. Remember, it is okay to make mistakes.

Reading

1. Read every day.
2. Use the visuals to help you figure out what words mean.
3. Reread parts that you do not understand.
4. Read many kinds of literature.
5. Ask for help.

Writing

1. Write something every day.
2. Plan your writing before you begin.
3. Read aloud what you write. Ask yourself whether it makes sense.
4. Check for spelling and grammar mistakes.

How to Study

Here are some tips for developing good study habits.

- **Schedule a time for studying.** It is easier to develop good study habits if you set aside the same time every day to study. Once you have a study routine, it will be easier for you to find time to prepare for larger projects or tests.

- **Create a special place for studying.** Find a study area where you are comfortable and where you have everything you need for studying. If possible, choose an area that is away from telephones or television. You can play music if it helps you to concentrate.

- **Read the directions first.** Make sure you understand what you are supposed to do. Ask a partner or your teacher about anything you do not understand.

- **Preview the reading.** Look at the pictures, illustrations, and captions in the reading. They will help you understand the text.

- **Learn unfamiliar words.** Try to figure out what unfamiliar words mean by finding context clues in the reading. If you still can't figure out the meaning, use a dictionary.

- **Take notes.** Keep notes in a notebook or journal of important things you want to remember from the reading.

- **Ask questions.** Write any questions you have from the reading. Discuss them with a partner or your teacher.

How to Build Vocabulary

Use these ideas to help you remember the meanings of new words.

Keep a Vocabulary Notebook Keep a notebook of vocabulary words and their definitions. Test yourself by covering either the word or the definition.

Make Flashcards On the front of an index card, write a word you want to remember. On the back, write the meaning. Use the cards to review the words with a partner or family member.

Say the Words Aloud Use your new words in sentences. Say the sentences to a partner or a family member.

How to Use a Book

The Title Page The title page states the title, the author, and the publisher.

The Table of Contents The table of contents is at the front of a book. The page on which a chapter begins is next to its name.

The Glossary The glossary is a small dictionary at the back of a book. It will tell you the meaning of a word and sometimes how to pronounce it. Use the glossary the same way you would use a dictionary.

The Index The index is at the back of a book. It lists subjects and names that are in the book, along with page numbers where you can find information.

The Bibliography The bibliography at the back of a book or chapter lets you know the books or sources where an author got information.

How to Use a Dictionary and Thesaurus

The Dictionary

You can find the **spelling**, **pronunciation**, **part of speech**, and **definitions** of words in the dictionary.

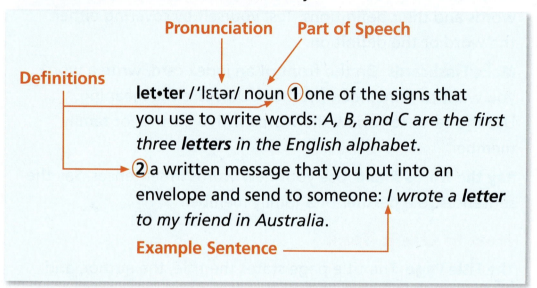

Pronunciation   Part of Speech

Definitions

let•ter /ˈlɛtər/ noun ① one of the signs that you use to write words: *A, B, and C are the first three **letters** in the English alphabet.*
② a written message that you put into an envelope and send to someone: *I wrote a **letter** to my friend in Australia.*

Example Sentence

The Thesaurus

A thesaurus is a specialized dictionary that lists **synonyms**, or words with similar meanings, and **antonyms**, or words with opposite meanings. Words in a thesaurus are arranged alphabetically. You can look up the word just as you would look it up in a dictionary.

Main entry: sad
Part of speech: adjective
Definition: unhappy
Synonyms: bitter, depressed, despairing, down, downcast, gloomy, glum, heartbroken, low, melancholy, morose, pessimistic, sorry, troubled, weeping
Antonyms: cheerful, happy

How to Take Tests

Taking tests is part of going to school. Use these tips to help you answer the kinds of questions you often see on tests.

True-False Questions

- If a statement seems true, make sure it is *all* true.
- The word *not* can change the meaning of a statement.
- Pay attention to words such as *all*, *always*, *never*, *no*, *none*, and *only*. They often make a statement false.
- Words such as *generally*, *much*, *many*, *sometimes*, and *usually* often make a statement true.

Multiple Choice Questions

- Try to answer the question before reading the choices. If your answer is one of the choices, choose it.
- Eliminate answers you know are wrong.
- Don't change your answer unless you know it is wrong.

Matching Questions

- Count each group to see whether any items will be left over.
- Read all the items before you start matching.
- Match the items you know first.

Fill-In-the-Blank Questions or Completions

- Read the question or incomplete sentence carefully.
- Look for clues in the question or sentence that might help you figure out the answer.
- If you are given possible answers, cross out each one as you use it.

Short Answers and Essays

- Take a few minutes to organize your thoughts.
- Give only the information that is asked for.
- Answer as clearly as possible.
- Leave time to proofread your response or essay.

Viewing and Representing Information

How to Read Maps and Diagrams

Informational texts often use maps, diagrams, graphs, and charts. These tools help illustrate and explain the topic.

Maps

Maps show the location of places such as countries, states, and cities. They can also show where mountains, rivers, lakes, and streets are located. A compass rose on the map shows which way is north. A scale shows how distances are represented on the map.

Diagrams

Diagrams are drawings that explain things or show how things work. Some diagrams show pictures of how objects look on the outside or on the inside. Others show the different steps in a process.

This diagram shows the steps of the Scientific Method. It helps you understand the order and importance of each step.

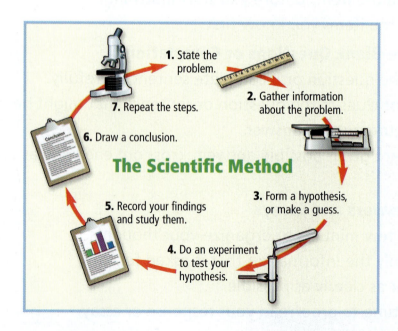

The Scientific Method

1. State the problem.
2. Gather information about the problem.
3. Form a hypothesis, or make a guess.
4. Do an experiment to test your hypothesis.
5. Record your findings and study them.
6. Draw a conclusion.
7. Repeat the steps.

How to Read Graphs

Graphs show how two or more kinds of information are related or alike. Three common kinds of graphs are **line graphs**, **bar graphs**, and **circle graphs**.

Line Graph

A **line graph** shows how information changes over a period of time. This line graph explains how the Native American population of Central Mexico changed over 120 years.

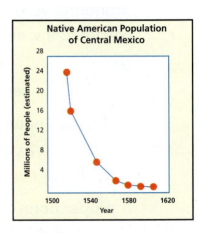

Bar Graphs

We use **bar graphs** to compare information. For example, this bar graph compares the populations of the 13 states that made up the U.S.A. in 1790.

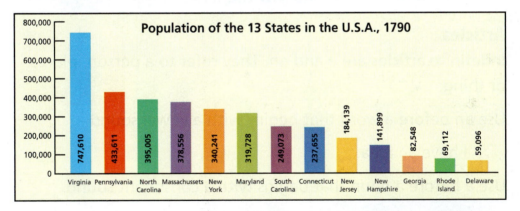

Circle Graphs

A **circle graph** is sometimes called a pie chart because it looks like a pie cut into slices. Circle graphs are used to show how different parts of a whole compare to each other.

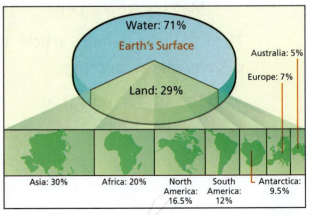

Grammar Handbook

Parts of Speech

In English there are nine **parts of speech**: nouns, articles, pronouns, verbs, adjectives, adverbs, prepositions, conjunctions, and interjections.

Nouns

Nouns name people, places, or things.

A **common noun** is a general person, place, or thing.

>   person   thing   place
> The **student** brings a **notebook** to **class**.

A **proper noun** is a specific person, place, or thing.

> person   place   thing
> **Joe** went to **Paris** and saw the **Eiffel Tower**.

Articles

Indefinite articles are *a* and *an*. They refer to a person, place, or thing.

Use *an* before a word that begins with a vowel sound.

> I have **an** idea.

Use *a* before a noun that begins with a consonant sound.

> May I borrow **a** pen?

The is called a **definite article**. Use *the* to talk about specific people, places, or things.

> **The** kitchen is next to **the** dining room.

Pronouns

Pronouns are words that take the place of nouns or proper nouns.

proper noun   pronoun
Ana is not home. **She** is babysitting.

	Subject Pronouns	Object Pronouns
Singular	I, you, he, she, it	me, you, him, her, it
Plural	we, you, they	us, you, them

A **subject pronoun** replaces the subject of a sentence. A **subject** is who or what a sentence is about.

subject   subject pronoun (singular)
Dan is a student. **He** goes to school every day.

Object pronouns replace a noun or proper noun that is the object of a verb. An **object** receives the action of a verb.

object   object pronoun (singular)

Lauren gave **Ed** the notes. Lauren gave **him** the notes.

Possessive pronouns replace nouns or proper nouns. They show who owns something.

	Possessive Pronouns
Singular	mine, yours, hers, his
Plural	ours, yours, theirs

Verbs

Verbs express an action or a state of being.

An **action verb** tells what someone or something does or did.

Verbs That Tell Actions You Can See	Verbs That Tell Actions You Cannot See
dance swim	know sense

A **linking verb** shows no action. It links the subject with another word that describes the subject.

Examples of Linking Verbs		
look	smell	sound
be	appear	seem

A helping verb comes before the main verb. It adds to the main verb's meaning.

	Helping Verbs
Forms of the verb *be*	am, is, was, were, being, been
Forms of the verb *do*	do, does, did
Forms of the verb *have*	have, has, had
Other helping verbs	can, must, could, have (to), should, may, will, would

Adjectives

Adjectives describe nouns. An adjective usually comes before the noun it describes.

tall grass   **big** truck

An adjective can come *after* the noun it describes. This often happens when the verb is a linking verb.

The bag is **heavy**. The books smell **new**.

Possessive adjectives describe who or what something belongs to.

possessive adjective
Someone saw **my/your/his/her/its/our/their** eyes.

Adverbs

Adverbs describe the action of verbs. They tell *how* an action happens. Adverbs answer the questions *Where?*, *When?*, *How?*, *How much?*, and *How often?*

Many adverbs end in *-ly*.

easily   slowly

Some adverbs do not end in *-ly*.

seldom   fast   very

In this sentence, the adverb *everywhere* modifies the verb *looked*. It answers the question *Where?*

verb   adverb
Nicole looked **everywhere** for her book.

Prepositions

Prepositions show time, place, and direction.

Time	Place	Direction
after	above	across
before	below	down

In this sentence, the preposition *above* shows where the bird flew. It shows place.

preposition

A bird flew **above** my head.

In this sentence, the preposition *across* shows direction.

preposition

The children walked **across** the street.

A **prepositional phrase** starts with a preposition and ends with a noun or pronoun. In this sentence, the preposition is *near* and the noun is *school*.

prepositional phrase

The library is **near the new school**.

Conjunctions

A **conjunction** joins words, groups of words, and whole sentences. Common conjunctions include *and*, *but*, and *or.*

The conjunction *and* joins two proper nouns: *Allison* and *Teresa*.

proper   proper
noun   noun

Allison **and** Teresa are in school.

The conjunction *or* joins two prepositional phrases: *to the movies* and *to the mall*.

prepositional   prepositional
phrase   phrase

They want to go to the movies **or** to the mall.

The conjunction *but* joins two independent clauses.

—— independent clause ——   —— independent clause ——

Alana baked the cookies, **but** Eric made the lemonade.

Interjections

Interjections are words or phrases that express emotion.

Interjections that express strong emotion are followed by an exclamation point.

    Wow! Did you see that goal?

A comma follows interjections that express mild emotion.

    Gee, I'm sorry that your team lost.

Sentences

Clauses

Clauses are groups of words with a subject and a verb.

- An **independent clause** can stand on its own as a complete sentence.
- A **dependent clause** cannot stand alone as a complete sentence.

Sentences

A simple sentence is an independent clause. It has a subject and a verb.

subject verb
The dog barked.

A **compound sentence** is made up of two or more simple sentences, or independent clauses.

┌─── independent clause ───┐ ┌─ independent clause ─┐
The band has a lead singer, **but** it needs a drummer.

Sentence Types

Declarative sentences are statements. They end with a period.

We are going to the beach on Saturday**.**

Interrogative sentences are questions. They end with a question mark.

Will you come with us**?**

Imperative sentences are commands. They end with a period or an exclamation point.

Put on your life jacket**.** Now jump in the water**!**

Exclamatory sentences express strong feeling. They end with an exclamation point.

I swam all the way from the boat to the shore**!**

Punctuation

End Marks

End marks come at the end of sentences. There are three kinds of end marks: periods, question marks, and exclamation points.

Periods

- Use a period to end a statement (declarative sentence).
- Use a period to end a command or request (imperative sentence).
- Use a period after a person's initial or abbreviated title.
- Use a period after abbreviations.

Question Marks and Exclamation Points

- Use an exclamation point to express strong feelings.
- Use a question mark at the end of a question.

Commas

Commas separate parts of a sentence or phrase.

- Use a comma to separate two independent clauses linked by a conjunction.
- Use commas to separate the parts in a series. A series is a group of three or more words, phrases, or clauses.
- Use a comma to set off introductory words or phrases.
- Use commas to set off an interrupting word or phrase.
- Use a comma to set off a speaker's quoted words.
- Use commas to set off the name of the person being addressed in a letter or speech.

Semicolons and Colons

Semicolons can connect two independent clauses. Use them when the clauses are closely related in meaning or structure.

Colons introduce a list of items or important information. Also use a colon to separate hours and minutes when writing the time.

Quotation Marks

Quotation marks set off direct quotations, dialogue, and some titles.

- Commas and periods always go inside quotation marks.
- If a question mark or exclamation point is not part of the quotation, it goes outside the quotation marks.
- Use quotation marks to set off what people say in a dialogue.
- Use quotation marks around the titles of short works of writing.

Apostrophes

Apostrophes can be used with singular and plural nouns to show ownership or possession. To form the possessive, follow these rules:

- For singular nouns, add an apostrophe and an *s*.
- For singular nouns that end in *s*, add an apostrophe and an *s*.
- For plural nouns that do not end in *s*, add an apostrophe and an *s*.
- For plural nouns that end in *s*, add an apostrophe.
- Apostrophes are also used in contractions to show where a letter or letters have been taken away.

Capitalization

There are five main reasons to use capital letters:

- to begin a sentence
- to write the pronoun *I*
- to write the names of proper nouns
- to write a person's title before his or her name
- to write the title of a work (artwork, written work)

Writing Handbook

Modes of Writing

Narrative Writing is used to tell a story. Here are some types of narrative writing:

- Autobiography is the story of a person's life told by the person.
- Biography is the story of a person's life told by another person.
- A short story is a short, fictional narrative.

Descriptive Writing paints a picture of a person, place, thing, or event.

Expository Writing gives information or explains something. Here are some types of expository writing:

- Compare-and-Contrast writing analyzes the similarities and differences between two or more things.
- Cause-and-Effect writing explains why something happened and what happens as a result.
- Problem-and-Solution writing describes a problem and offers one or more solutions to it.
- How-to writing explains how to do or make something.

Persuasive Writing is writing that tries to convince people to think or act in a certain way.

Functional Writing is writing for real-world uses. Here are some types of functional writing:

- You might fill out a form to sign up for lessons, take a field trip, or apply for a library card.
- You might create an invitation to a holiday party.

The Writing Process

The writing process is a series of steps that helps you write clearly.

Step 1: Prewrite

When you prewrite, you explore ideas and choose a topic. You identify your audience, and you choose your purpose for writing.

To choose a topic, try one or more of these strategies:
- **List** many ideas that you might want to write about.
- **Freewrite** about some ideas for five minutes.
- **Brainstorm** a list of ideas with a partner.

To identify your audience, think about who will read your writing. What do they already know? What do you need to explain?

To identify your purpose for writing, ask:
- Do I want to entertain my audience?
- Do I want to inform my audience?
- Do I want to persuade my audience?

Now, decide on the best form for your writing. Gather and organize the details that will support your topic.

Step 2: Draft

You start writing in this step. Put your ideas into sentences. Put your sentences into paragraphs. Begin to put your paragraphs in order. Don't worry too much about grammar and spelling. You will have a chance to correct any errors later.

Step 3: Revise

This is the time to look at your ideas and the organization of your writing. Read your first draft. Ask yourself:

- Are the ideas presented in the best order?
- Is there a clear beginning, middle, and end?
- Does each paragraph have a main idea and supporting details?

Decide what changes you will make. Then revise your draft.

Step 4: Edit/Proofread

This is the time to look at word choice, sentence fluency, and writing conventions. Reread your paper. Proofread for mistakes in spelling, grammar, and punctuation. Correct any mistakes you find.

When you edit and proofread your draft, use the proofreading marks in the chart below to mark the changes.

Editing/Proofreading Marks		
To:	**Use This Mark:**	**Example:**
add something	$\wedge$	We ate rice, bean, and corn.
delete something	ℓ	We ate rice, beans, and corns.
start a new paragraph	¶	¶ We ate rice, beans, and corn.
add a comma	ˏ	We ate rice, beans and corn.
add a period	⊙	We ate rice, beans, and corn⊙
switch letters or words	∼	We ate rice, baens, and corn.
change to a capital letter	a̲	we ate rice, beans, and corn.
change to a lowercase letter	Ⱥ	WE ate rice, beans, and corn.

Peer Review Checklist

Ideas

☐ Is the content interesting and thoughtful?

☐ Is the main idea clearly stated?

☐ Are the main ideas supported by facts and details?

☐ Do the ideas flow from one to the next?

Organization

☐ Are the ideas in an order that makes sense?

☐ Are the ideas connected by transitions and other connecting words?

Voice

☐ Does the writing have energy and personality?

Word Choice

☐ Has the writer chosen precise words?

Sentence Fluency

☐ Do the sentences flow smoothly?

☐ Are the sentences varied in type and length?

Conventions

☐ Do the subjects of sentences agree with the verbs?

☐ Do the pronouns agree with the words they refer to?

☐ Are the verb tenses appropriate and consistent?

☐ Is the possessive case (apostrophe -s) used correctly?

☐ Are negatives and contractions used correctly?

☐ Are the punctuation and capitalization correct?

☐ Is the writing free of spelling errors?

Once you have revised and proofread your paper, share it with others. Look at these publishing ideas:

- Post your paper on the bulletin board.
- Photocopy your paper. Hand it out to your classmates and family members.
- Attach it to an email and send it to friends.
- Send it to a school newspaper or magazine for possible publication.

Once you have shared your work with others, you may want to put it in your portfolio. A portfolio is a folder or envelope in which you keep your writing. If you keep your work in a portfolio, you can look at what you have written over a period of time. This will let you see if your writing is improving. It will help you become a better writer.

Build Your Portfolio

You may want to keep your completed writing in your portfolio. It is a good idea to keep your drafts, too. Keep comments you receive from your teacher or writing partner, as well.

Reflect on Your Writing

Make notes on your writing in a journal. Write how you felt about what you wrote. Use these questions to help you get started:

- What new things did you learn about your topic?
- What helped you organize the details in your writing?
- What helped you revise your writing?
- What did you learn about yourself as you wrote?

Rubric for Writing

A rubric is a tool that helps you assess, or evaluate, your work. This rubric shows specific details for you to think about when you write. The scale ranges from 4 to 1, with 4 being the highest score and 1 being the lowest.

4	Writing is clearly focused on the task. Writing is well organized. Ideas follow a logical order. Main idea is fully developed and supported with details. Sentence structure is varied. Writing is free of fragments. There are no errors in writing conventions.
3	Writing is focused, but with some unnecessary information. There is clear organization, but with some ideas out of order. The main idea is supported, but development is uneven. Sentence structure is mostly varied, but with some fragments. Writing conventions are generally followed.
2	Writing is related to the task, but lacks focus. Organization is not clear. Ideas do not fit well together. There is little or no support for the main idea. No variation in sentence structure. Fragments occur often. Frequent errors in writing conventions.
1	The writing is generally unfocused. There is little organization or development. There is no clear main idea. Sentence structure is unvaried. There are many fragments. Many errors in writing conventions and spelling.

Writing and Research

Sometimes when you write, you need to do research to learn more information about your topic. You can do research in the library, on the Internet, and by viewing or listening to information media.

Library Reference

Encyclopedias contain basic facts, background information, and suggestions for additional research.

Biographical references provide brief life histories of famous people in many different fields.

Almanacs contain facts and statistics about many subjects, including government, world history, geography, entertainment, business, and sports.

Periodicals are past editions of magazines. Use a periodical index to find articles on your topic.

Vertical files contain pamphlets on a wide variety of topics.

Electronic databases provide quick access to information on many topics.

Citing Sources

When you do research, you read what other people wrote. The material you research is called the source, or reference. When you tell who wrote the material, this is called citing the source. It is important to cite each source you use when you write.

In your paper, note each place in which you use a source. At the end of the paper, provide a list that gives details about all your sources. A bibliography and a works cited list are two types of source lists.

- A **bibliography** provides a listing of all the material you used during your research.
- A **works cited list** shows the sources you have quoted in your paper.

Plagiarism

Plagiarism is presenting someone else's words, ideas, or work as your own. If the idea or words are not yours, be sure to give credit by citing the source in your work. It is a serious offense to plagiarize.

Look at the chart of the Modern Language Association (MLA) on p. 407. Use this format for citing sources. This is the most common format for papers written by middle and high school students, as well as college students.

MLA Style for Listing Sources

Book	Ormiston, Rosalind. *Origins of Modern Art.* London: Flame Tree Publishing, 2015.
Article in a magazine	"He Had a Dream." *Scholastic News* 8 Jan. 2018: 4–5.
Films and DVDs	*Coco.* Dir. Lee Unkrich. Perf. Anthony Gonzalez, Gael García Bernal, Benjamin Bratt, Alanna Ubach, Renée Victor, Ana Ofelia Murguía, and Edward James Olmos. Walt Disney Studios Motion Picture, 2017.
Internet	Green, James. *Beadwork in the Arts of Africa and Beyond.* July 26, 2018. www.metmuseum.org/blogs/collection-insights/2018/beadwork-in-arts-of-africa-and-beyond. Accessed August 21, 2018.
Newspaper	Bowles, Scott. "Ready to Roll at Comic-Con." *USA Today* 22 July 2009: D1 Print.
Personal interview	Smith, Jane. Personal interview. 10 Feb. 2018.

Internet Research

The internet is an international network of computers. The World Wide Web is a part of the internet that lets you find and read information.

To do research on the internet, you need to open a search engine. Type in a keyword on the search engine page. **Keywords** are words or phrases on the topic you want to learn about. For example, if you are looking for information about your favorite musical group, you might use the band's name as a keyword.

To choose a keyword, write a list of all the words you are considering. Then choose a few of the most important words.

Tips

- Spell the keywords correctly.
- Use the most important keyword first, followed by the less important ones.
- Open the pages at the top of the list first. These will usually be the most useful sources.

How to Evaluate Information from the Internet

When you do research on the internet, you need to be sure the information is correct. Use the checklist to decide if you can trust the information on a Web site.

✔ Look at the address bar. A URL that ends in "edu" is connected to a school or university. A URL that ends in "gov" means it is a site posted by a state or federal government. These sites should have correct information.

✔ Check that the people who write or are quoted on the site are experts, not just people telling their ideas or opinions.

✔ Check that the site is free of grammatical and spelling errors. This is often a hint that the site was carefully designed and researched.

✔ Check that the site is not trying to sell a product or persuade people.

✔ If you are not sure about using a site as a source, ask an adult.

Information Media

Media is all the organizations that provide news and information to the public. Media includes television, radio, and newspapers. This chart describes several forms of information media.

Types of Information Media	
Television News Program	• Covers current news events • Gives information objectively
Documentary	• Focuses on one topic of social interest • Sometimes expresses controversial opinions
Television Newsmagazine	• Covers a variety of topics • Entertains and informs
Radio Talk Show	• Covers some current events • Offers a place for people to express opinions
Newspaper Article	• Covers one current event • Gives details and background about the event
Commercial	• Presents products, people, or ideas • Persuades people to buy or take action

How to Evaluate Information from Various Media

Because the media presents large amounts of information, it is important to learn how to analyze this information. Some media sources try to make you think a certain way instead of giving you all the facts. Use these techniques to figure out whether you can trust information from the media.

✔ Sort facts from opinions. A fact is a statement that can be proven true. An opinion is how someone feels or thinks about something. Make sure any opinions are supported by facts.

✔ Be aware of the kind of media you are watching, reading, or listening to. Is it news or a documentary? Is it a commercial? What is its purpose?

✔ Watch out for bias. **Bias** is when the source gives information from only one point of view. Try to gather information from several points of view.

✔ Discuss what you learn from different media with your classmates or teachers. This will help you determine if you can trust the information.

✔ Read the entire article or watch the whole program before reaching a conclusion. Then develop your own views on the issues, people, and information presented.

How To Use Technology in Writing

Writing on a Computer

You can write using a word-processing program. This will help you when you follow the steps in the Writing Process.

- When you write your first draft, save it as a document.
- As you type or revise, you can move words and sentences using the cut, copy, and paste commands.
- When you proofread, you can use the grammar and spell-check functions to help you check your work.

Keeping a Portfolio

Create folders to save your writing in. For example, a folder labeled "Writing Projects—September" can contain all of the writing you do during that month.

Save all the drafts of each paper you write.

Computer Tips

- Rename each of your revised drafts using the SAVE AS function. For example, if your first draft is "Cats," name the second draft "Cats2."
- If you share your computer, create a folder for only your work.
- Always back up your portfolio on a server or a USB flash drive.

accident → caves

A

accident something that happens unexpectedly (p. 230)

advertise make people aware of and interested in an event or product (p. 324)

affect produce a change (p. 88)

alternative different from something else (p. 356)

amazing very surprising and exciting (p. 136)

annual happening every year (p. 326)

appreciate like or understand the value of something (p. 138)

assign give a duty or task (p. 262)

attitude a way of thinking (p. 88)

B

bark the outer covering of a tree (p. 276)

benefit helped by (p. 198)

bicycles vehicles with two wheels that you sit on and ride by moving your legs (p. 196)

billions at least twice more than the number 1,000,000,000 (p. 260)

brighter more sunny; having more light (p. 86)

butterfly insect that has large wings with bright colors on them (p. 166)

buttons small round objects that you push through a hole to fasten (p. 338)

C

camels animals with long necks and one or two humps on their backs (p. 136)

camouflage act of hiding something by making it look the same as the things around it (p. 152)

canoe narrow, light boat that you move using a paddle (p. 276)

caterpillar young form of some insects, that looks like a worm with many tiny legs (p. 166)

cause something that makes an action happen (p. 354)

caves hollow places under the ground or in the side of a mountain (p. 136)

celebrate have a special meal or party because of a particular event (p. 38)

clouds masses of very small drops of water floating in the sky (p. 86)

company a person or people you are with (p. 38)

consist of be made up of (p. 262)

continents the large areas of land on Earth, such as Africa, Europe, and Australia (p. 260)

contribute give something (p. 40)

craters round holes in the ground made by something that has fallen or exploded on them (p. 260)

create make something (pp. 24, 354)

creation something that is made (p. 230)

crowd large groups of people (p. 38)

dessert sweet food that you eat at the end of a meal (p. 22)

dinner main meal of the day, usually eaten in the evening (p. 72)

discover find something by accident (p. 230)

donate give something to a person or organization that needs help (p. 196)

enable make someone or something able to do something (p. 154)

environment world of land, sea, and air that something lives in (p. 154)

farm a place to grow food (p. 104)

festival a time of celebration; a program of cultural events (p. 324)

flight trip in an airplane or space craft (p. 290)

flower part of the plant that has the seeds and is brightly colored (p. 8)

focus pay attention to (p. 74)

fold bend a piece of paper or cloth so that one part covers the other (p. 22)

fresh recently grown (p. 104)

friend person you like and trust very much (p. 22)

garden piece of land where flowers or vegetables are grown around a house or in a public place (p. 104)

gathers comes together in a group (p. 38)

goal something you want to achieve (p. 356)

greet welcome someone (p. 8)

grow develop into food (p. 104)

habitats natural places where plants or animals live (p. 152)

habits things that you always do, often without thinking about it (p. 136)

handprints marks on a surface that are made by a hand or hands (p. 276)

hatch come out of an egg (p. 166)

helmets hard hats that cover and protect your head (p. 196)

identify tell what something is (p. 74)

illustrate show; make something clear by giving examples (p. 138)

immigrate enter another country in order to live there (p. 292)

imply say something in an indirect way (p. 232)

insect very small creature such as a fly, that has six legs (p. 152)

instinct natural ability to behave in a particular way without having to think about it or learn it (p. 214)

interact communicate; talk to other people and work together with them (p. 106)

invented created something new (p. 230)

item single piece or thing (p. 10)

lab room or building in which a scientist works (p. 214)

leaf one of the flat green parts of a plant or tree that grow out of branches or a stem (p. 166)

letter a written message (p. 8)

luck good and bad things that happen to you by chance (p. 8)

method a way of doing something (p. 216)

mix put different things together to make something new; join together (p. 22)

moth insect like a butterfly that flies at night (p. 152)

normally most of the time (p. 198)

observe watch someone or something carefully (p. 290)

occurs happens; takes place (p. 168)

outcome the final result of a meeting, process, etc. (p. 106)

participate be involved in (p. 326)

patterns arrangements of shapes, lines, or colors (p. 152)

phenomenon something we can observe, or see; something that is out of the ordinary (p. 278)

plains large areas of flat lands (p. 136)

planets large objects in space like Earth that move around a star such as the sun (p. 260)

plants living things that have leaves and roots (p. 104)

prey animal that is hunted and eaten by another animal (p. 152)

proof facts that prove something is true (p. 214)

public people in a community (p. 354)

puppets small figures of people or animals that you can move by pulling the strings, or by putting your hand inside them (p. 338)

purchase buy (p. 10)

quilt soft thick cover for a bed (p. 230)

rainbow large curve of different colors that appears in the sky after it rains (p. 276)

reflection what you see in a mirror or similar surface (p. 72)

required something needed (p. 340)

reverse backward; opposite way (p. 340)

roars makes a deep loud noise (p. 72)

rotates turns around a fixed point (p. 260)

satellite object sent into space to receive signals from one part of the world and send them to another (p. 290)

schedule plan of what you will do and when you will do it (p. 324)

scientists people who study or work in science (p. 214)

scissors instrument with two sharp blades joined together used for cutting paper, cloth, etc. (p. 338)

significant important (p. 292)

similar almost the same, but not quite (p. 40)

solve figure out a problem (p. 230)

space shuttle type of vehicle that can carry people into space and then return to Earth to be used again (p. 290)

spacewalks moving around outside a space craft while in space (p. 290)

sphere solid round shape like a ball (p. 260)

spiders small creatures with eight legs that use threads from their bodies to make webs (p. 86)

stapler tool used for putting in staples to hold pieces of paper together (p. 338)

statement something that is said aloud (p. 354)

street a road in a town or city with buildings next to it (p. 8)

stronger having more power or force (p. 86)

supplies things that are needed to carry out a task or activity (p. 324)

symbol something that stands for an idea (pp. 232, 355)

tadpole small creature that lives in the water and becomes a frog or toad (p. 166)

task job that must be done (p. 24)

theory unproven idea that explains something (p. 216)

tool thing that helps you build or repair other things (p. 214)

traditional following ideas or methods that have existed for a long time (p. 278)

transform completely change (p. 168)

volunteers people who offer to do things without expecting to be paid (p. 196)

webs nets of sticky thin threads made by spiders (p. 86)

weekend Saturday and Sunday (p. 38)

well a deep hole in the ground from which water is taken (p. 72)

yarn thick thread used by someone to knit something (p. 338)

Credits

Shutterstock; 087 (TR) Mirvav/Shutterstock; 087 (BL) LouLouPhotos/Shutterstock; 087 (BR) Mesto Sveta/Shutterstock; 088 Darrin Henry/Shutterstock; 098 Lopolo/Shutterstock; 102 Artisticco/Shutterstock; 103 Dan Kosmayer/Shutterstock; 104 Didier Zylberyng/Alamy Stock Photo; 104 (Inset) Steve Cukrov/Shutterstock; 106 Myrleen Pearson/Alamy Stock Photo; 108 Anton Watman/Shutterstock; 108–113 (Bkgrd) Jitlada Panwiset/Shutterstock; 109 Alison Hancock/Shutterstock; 110 Didier Zylberyng/Alamy Stock Photo; 111 Bloomberg/Getty Images; 112 RJ Sangosti/Denver Post/Getty Images; 114 Jitlada Panwiset/Shutterstock; 115 Gillmar/Shutterstock; 117 Steve Debenpor/E+/Getty Images; 119 Monkey Business Images/Shutterstock; 121 Ariel Skelley/Digital Vision/Getty Images; 123 Hill Street Studios/Blend Images/Getty Images; 126 Berangere Duforets/123RF.

UNIT 3: 130–131 Volodymyr Burdiak/Shutterstock; 130 (L) Damsea/Shutterstock; 130 (C) Donna A. Herrmann/Shutterstock; 130 (R) Cal Vornberger/Alamy Stock Photo; 133 (TL) Andreas Zerndl/Shutterstock; 133 (TR) Xfdly/Shutterstock; 133 (B) Sittitap/Shutterstock; 134 (L) Claudio De Rubertis/Shutterstock; 134 (L Inset) Kevin Dodge/Blend Images/Getty Images; 134 (R) D. Kucharski K. Kucharska/Shutterstock; 134 (R Inset) Monkey Business Images/Shutterstock; 135 (TR) Matee Nuserm/123RF; 135 (TR Inset) SolStock/E+/Getty Images; 135 (BL) Anuradha Marwah/Shutterstock; 135 (BL Inset) Dreet Production/Alloy/Getty Images; 136 (T) Aleksandr Frolov/123RF; 136 (B) Agnieszka Bacal/Shutterstock; 137 (TL) Jaimie Duplass/Shutterstock; 137 (TR) Dieter H/Shutterstock; 137 (BR) Prisma by Dukas Presseagentur GmbH/Alamy Stock Photo; 138 Holbox/Shutterstock; 139 Brandon Alms/Shutterstock; 140 (T) Damsea/Shutterstock; 140 (B) Liquid Light/iStock/Getty Images; 141 (Bkgrd) John Pitcher/iStock/Getty Images; 141 (Inset) Andrey Armyagov/123RF; 144 (TL) Eddie Sylvester/123RF; 144 (TR) NASA Photo/Alamy Stock Photo; 144 (BL) Michael J Thompson/Shutterstock; 144 (BR) Evelyng23/Shutterstock; 145 (TL) Mohammed Anwarul Kabir Choudhury/123RF; 145 (TR) Tamara321/Shutterstock; 145 (B) Joshua Rainey Photography/Shutterstock; 146 Charles Brutlag/123RF; 147 NASA Photo/Alamy Stock Photo; 149 Arco Images GmbH/G. Lacz/Alamy Stock Photo; 151 Boonchuay Promjiam/Shutterstock; 153 (T) Blickwinkel/Alamy Stock Photo; 153 (B) Henrik Larsson/Shutterstock; 154 Delmas Lehman/Shutterstock; 155 Eileen Kumpf/Shutterstock; 156 (T) Jack Hong/Shutterstock; 156 (C Inset) Vladimir Melnik/Shutterstock; 156 (B) Seokhee Kim/Shutterstock; 157 (T) Chris Watson/Shutterstock; 157 (B) DJ Taylor/Shutterstock; 158 (T) Jason Mintzer/Shutterstock; 158 (BL) Danyu/Shutterstock; 158 (CR) Mihir Joshi/Shutterstock; 159 (T) Artush/123RF; 159 (B) Donna A. Herrmann/Shutterstock; 160 Mihir Joshi/Shutterstock; 161 Seokhee Kim/Shutterstock; 163 Natali Glado/Shutterstock; 165 Brian Lasenby/Shutterstock; 167 (T) Carlos Huang/Shutterstock; 166 (a) Thammanoon Khamchalee/Shutterstock; 166 (b) Survivalphotos/Alamy Stock Photo; 166 (C) Cathy Keifer/Shutterstock; 166 (d) Thomas Kitchin & Victoria Hurst/Design Pics Inc/Alamy Stock Photo; 166 (e) Kingfisher/Shutterstock; 166 (f) Del/Monaco/Shutterstock; 166 (T) James Laurie/Shutterstock; 167 (B) D. Kucharski K. Kucharska/Shutterstock; 168 Best Photo Plus/Shutterstock; 169 Fuyu liu/Shutterstock; 170 (T) Hugh Lansdown/Shutterstock; 170 (B) Jason Ross/123RF; 171 (TL) Hugh Lansdown/Shutterstock; 171 (a) Alen thien/Shutterstock; 171 (b) Andrew Waugh/Alamy Stock Photo; 171 (c) Photoncatcher/123RF; 171 (d) Altair/Shutterstock; 172 (T) Steve Byland/Shutterstock; 172 (CL) Przemyslaw Muszynski/Shutterstock; 172 (CR) Carlos Huang/Shutterstock; 172 (B) FLPA/Alamy Stock Photo; 173 Thomas Marent/Rolf Nussbaumer Photography/Alamy Stock Photo; 174 (T) Carlos Huang/Shutterstock; 174 (B) Dr. Morley Read/Shutterstock; 175

Images; 271 Interfoto/Alamy Stock Photo; 272 NikoNomad/Shutterstock; 275 NikoNomad/Shutterstock; 276 (TL) Michael Richardson/Shutterstock; 276 (TC) Reinhold Leitner/Shutterstock; 276 (TR) Knelson20/ Shutterstock; 276 (BL) Zaitsava Olga/ Shutterstock; 276 (BR) Lucian Milasan/123RF; 277 (T) Ariel Skelley/Digital Vision/ Getty Images; 277 (B) Ignacio Salaverria/ Shutterstock; 278 Atiketta Sangasaeng/ Shutterstock; 279 (T) Reinhold Leitner/ Shutterstock; 279 (B) Alexei_tm/Shutterstock; 286 Kdshutterman/Shutterstock; 289 NASA; 290 (T) NASA; 290 (B) StockTrek/Purestock/ Alamy Stock Photo; 291 (L) Babak Tafreshi/ National Geographic Creative/Alamy Stock Photo; 291 (R) NASA; 292 Wavebreakmedia/ Shutterstock; 293 EduardHarkonen/ iStock/Getty Images; 294 NASA; 295 EduardHarkonen/iStock/Getty Images; 296 Sergey Nivens/Shutterstock; 297 Philip Scalia/ Alamy Stock Photo; 298 NASA; 299 Gmutlu/ Photographer's Choice RF/Getty Images; 300 (TL) NASA; 300 (TR) AbleStock.com/Getty Images; 300 (BL) NASA; 300 (BR) NASA; 301 (TL) NG Images/Alamy Stock Photo; 301 (TR) JPL/USGS/NASA; 301 (B) Interfoto/ Alamy Stock Photo; 302 NASA; 303 NASA; 305 KK Tan/Shutterstock; 308 Kdshutterman/ Shutterstock; 311 Vadim Sadovski/ Shutterstock; 314 Khakimullin Aleksandr/ Shutterstock.

UNIT 6: 318–319 Thirteen/Shutterstock; 318 (L) Kali Antye/Shutterstock; 318 (R) Cavan Images/Cavan/Getty Images; 321 (TL) Aberration/123RF; 321 (TR) Studio 8/Pearson Education Ltd; 321 (BL) Billion Photos/ Shutterstock; 321 (BR) SeDmi/Shutterstock; 322 (L) Chattanooga Times Free Press, Doug Strickland/AP Images; 322 (L Inset) Anna Nahabed/Shutterstock; 322 (R) Martyn Goddard/Alamy Stock Photo; 322 (R Inset) Monkey Business Images/Shutterstock; 323 (T) Michael Willis/Alamy Stock Photo; 323 (T Inset) Monkey Business Images/Shutterstock; 323 (B) Tuul and Bruno Morandi/Alamy Stock Photo; 323 (B Inset) Rawpixel.com/

Shutterstock; 324 Vandame/Shutterstock; 325 Woodys Photos/Shutterstock; 326 Cheuk-king Lo/Pearson Education Asia Ltd; 327 Studio 8/Pearson Education Ltd; 328 OpopO/Shutterstock; 330 Mediaphotos/ E+/Getty Images; 332 Shironosov/iStock/ Getty Images; 333 Lightfieldstudios/123RF; 335 Luis Echeverri Urrea/Shutterstock; 338 (T) Stephen Coburn/Shutterstock; 338 (CL) Zvyagintsev Sergey/Shutterstock; 338 (CR) Buntoon Rodseng/123RF; 338 (B) Bialasiewicz/123RF; 339 (TL) Shironosov/ iStock/Getty Images; 339 (TR) Nordling/ Shutterstock; 339 (C) Sidekick/E+/Getty Images; 339 (B) Donatas1205/Shutterstock; 340 Creativestockexchange/Shutterstock; 342 Bogdan Ionescu/Shutterstock; 343 (TL) Mayuree Moonhirun/Shutterstock; 343 (TR) Artjom Shipilov/Shutterstock; 343 (CL) Denis and Yulia Pogostins/Shutterstock; 343 (C) Yaroslav Domnitsky/123RF; 343 (CR) Alexandkz/123RF; 343 (BCL) Vecta/ Shutterstock; 343 (BCR) Evlakhov Valeriy/ Shutterstock; 343 (BL) George P. Choma/ Shutterstock; 343 (BC) Pixelfeger/ Shutterstock; 343 (BR) Garsya/Shutterstock; 344 (T) Mega Pixel/Shutterstock; 344 (T Inset) Yaroslav Domnitsky/123RF; 344 (CL) Mayuree Moonhirun/Shutterstock; 344 (CR) Wavebreak Media Ltd/123RF; 344 (BL) Creativestockexchange/Shutterstock; 344 (BR) Evlakhov Valeriy/Shutterstock; 344 (B Inset) Allen Eyestone/The Palm Beach Post/ ZUMAPRESS.com/Alamy Stock Photo; 345 (T) Africa Studio/Shutterstock; 345 (BL) Denis and Yulia Pogostins/Shutterstock; 345 (BR) Kali Antye/Shutterstock; 346 (TL) Dallas and John Heaton/Travel Pictures/Alamy Stock Photo; 346 (TR) Iwona Grodzka/Shutterstock; 346 (B) Chee-Onn Leong/Shutterstock; 347 (TL) Xinhua/Alamy Stock Photo; 347 (TR) Hugh Threlfall/Alamy Stock Photo; 347 (B) Sol Stock/E+/Getty Images; 348 (T) Wavebreak Media Ltd/123RF; 348 (B) Allen Eyestone/ The Palm Beach Post/ZUMAPRESS.com/Alamy Stock Photo; 351 Dado Photos/Shutterstock; 353 Everett Collection Inc/Alamy Stock Photo; 354 (T) Anastasiia Boriagina/123RF;